THINKING ALOUD

THINKING ALOUD

Reflections on Emerging India

PRASOON JOSHI

RUPA

Published by
Rupa Publications India Pvt. Ltd 2019
7/16, Ansari Road, Daryaganj
New Delhi 110002

Sales centres:
Allahabad Bengaluru Chennai
Hyderabad Jaipur Kathmandu
Kolkata Mumbai

Copyright © Prasoon Joshi 2019
The Acknowledgements (on page 193) is an extension of
the copyright page.

The views and opinions expressed in this book are the author's own and the facts are as reported by him which have been verified to the extent possible, and the publishers are not in any way liable for the same.

While every effort has been made by the editor to trace copyright holders and obtain permission, this has not been possible in all cases; any omissions brought to our attention will be remedied in future editions.

All rights reserved.
No part of this publication may be reproduced, transmitted, or stored in a retrieval system, in any form or by any means, electronic, mechanical, photocopying, recording or otherwise, without the prior permission of the publisher.

ISBN: 978-93-5304-597-5

First impression 2019

10 9 8 7 6 5 4 3 2 1

The moral right of the author has been asserted.

Printed by Parksons Graphics Pvt. Ltd., Mumbai

This book is sold subject to the condition that it shall not, by way of trade or otherwise, be lent, resold, hired out, or otherwise circulated, without the publisher's prior consent, in any form of binding or cover other than that in which it is published.

Contents

Prologue   *vii*

SECTION 1: CULTURAL LAYERS
1. Culture and Counterculture   3
2. The Uncommon Saga of the Common Man   10
3. Are We Free Thinkers?   16
4. Why Such Violentainment?   21
5. Social Walls: Demolish Convenient Windows for the Real View   28
6. Post-truth: The Fiction About Fact   34
7. Surrogacy Saga: Looking for a Silver Lining   40

SECTION 2: THINKING UNPLUGGED
8. Material Branding of the Abstract: Real Art, Packaged Products and the Thin Line   49
9. Creativity in Adversity   54
10. Ideas: The Liminal Space   60
11. Asian Creativity: Indefinable, Limitless   63

12. The New Frontier: Creativity in the
    Changing Times   67
13. Artificial Intelligence and Advait   74
14. Art and Responsibility: Is Art Independent of
    Societal Constraints?   80

SECTION 3: VOID AND CELLULOID
15. Fundamentals of Entertainment Products   91
16. Bollywood: A Spectacle Beyond Entertainment?   98
17. The Melodies of Life   104
18. A Peek into the Hundred Years of Indian Cinema   122
19. Romance in Hindi Cinema: Reverence and
    Realism in Film Songs   127

SECTION 4: HEAR IT ECHO
20. Art of Communication: Neurons,
    Gigabytes and Gaps   137
21. When Will Indian Advertising Go Global?   147
22. Unreal World of Advertising!   157
23. Advertising: Allure and Accountability   161
24. Promotions in an Indian Context   166
25. Women in Indian Ads: From Selling Products to
    Leading Change   170
26. Rituals: A Powerful Brand Asset   176
27. Subliminal Messaging: An Underused Tool   181
28. Good Begets Good: Consumption with
    Compassion   187

Acknowledgements   193

Prologue

Life, for me, is a vantage point. Things exist as they are—fluid, amorphous. It's a frame of mind, an individual interpretation that gives form and makes them unique. A river is perceived differently when viewed from diverse points. From a river bank, one watches it ebb and flow; from a hillock, another sees it gracefully meander; for yet another who dips into it, the surge and current are intense. To each one, the same river has a different meaning, defined by their individual experience.

A vantage point—layered as it is with various experiences, metaphors and symbols—is authentic, one of its kind. And an authentic perspective is central to my being. For, there is no substitute for first-hand experience. If one has felt and sensed in full measure, the understanding is deep and nuanced. As the degrees of separation increase from the experience, original layers tend to get lost, or other, often unwarranted ones, get added.

Putting the authentic into play is not always effortless, for there is a tendency in us to selectively enforce a previously felt emotion. It requires a true seeker to constantly unpeel and reach the core. This process is granular, for each sentiment that is stirred is organic, original. It is this felt reality—the 'anubhoot satya'—and its expression, which hails supreme for me. It's this experienced truth which compels me to pick up my pen.

Sometimes though, the single lens of self-experience is not forthcoming. Yet, a perspective emerges, probably because there exists a filter or two through which one consumes a certain reality. It's about having, what I term as a 'Cultural eye' or 'Organism (Creature) eye'. Let me try and elaborate. If there's a cultural underpinning, one reacts from a particular vantage point and through a particular lens—which is the sum total of one's visual library, experiences and sensorial learning. Take for example, a woman walking at a distance, with a distinct red colour visible on her forehead. For one who is familiar with Indian culture, it would probably imply tradition, 'sindoor', married. However, for another who is sans this filter, from a distance it could be a woman with a wound, a trickle of blood oozing from the forehead. A culturally nuanced figure of speech, visual or cuisine requires a certain familiarity filter.

Conversely, when a thought, expression or gesture has no reference point or filter which makes it palatable, the Organism eye kicks in. The Organism eye is primal; it works in conjunction with the baser instincts, and consumes and deciphers the overt.

Take, for instance, a film like *Jurassic Park*. One doesn't need a specific cultural context to connect; the basic aspects of fear and survival are relatable. Each person will have their own filter or a way of framing an experience. For me, it's about a unique viewpoint: How you see the same reality differently is where creativity comes in. It's the eye that is new. Creativity, a fresh perspective and life are intertwined.

In the fields of communication and entertainment, my filters of a Cultural eye and Organism eye have helped me understand content from across the world, from divergent minds and cultures. I have been able to soak in the so-called high art from France and street art from Brazilian favelas, delve into folk music as well as Sanskrit poetry, engage in Luis Buñuel and Alejandro González Iñárritu's cinematic points of view, and create a fertile ground for my experiences to morph into expression.

Though I write continually—be it poetry, scripts, short stories and communication campaigns—along the way, writing articles became of consequence to me. Writing a book or a feature film has a certain gestation period, a longer journey to undertake. Penning articles is more immediate and propels me to explore spontaneously and observe attentively.

Often, the everyday becomes part of the backdrop, or it simply ceases to exist. The wondrous strands of the usual stand neglected just because the common is constant. To set eyes on the familiar with a fresh perspective, streamline scattered ideas and delve deeper into the genesis of the seemingly ordinary—writing articles became my rafts for such shorter voyages. They provided a means to reach out and share the here and now of a given context.

Of course, the canvas of an article is limited. It seems an issue or thought is touched upon, not unraveled fully; like the light has flickered, not shone entirely. But then, at times, it may not be possible for the fog to lift completely— just important to see through it. Articles, for me, are such capsules of contemplation.

This book is a collection of some articles written over the last decade or so, most of them published in various dailies or magazines. They stem from thoughts I stumbled upon whilst working and interacting on various projects, films, forums, literature festival discussions and so forth. Some of them are set earlier in the decade, reflecting a simpler context, and the recent ones are of a more complex weave.

As shafts of light from various sources help to only further illuminate an object on which they fall, the points I have raised or areas I have ventured into, represent my take, and attempt to cast a humble shaft of thought on them. By no means do I claim to be an authority on any of the subjects, be it culture dynamics, gender studies, cinema, linguistics or communication. This book is simply about taking the liberty to look at them from my vantage point. I consider myself 'work-in-progress', for one's thoughts constantly evolve and get shaped as life surges on. All I try is to be open to diverse ideas and thoughts. My intention is to share a perspective and evoke thought, and through a process of introspection and internal churn, understand the change around us in terms of both, the personal and the collective. After all, art, society, industry, systems, freedom and responsibilities are contextual and work-in-progress—like ourselves.

Prasoon Joshi

SECTION 1

Cultural Layers

A life sans culture will be mechanical. Culture gives us a context for life. A mundane object finds meaning and significance because we decide to attribute a narrative to it. Societies prize and cherish their narratives dearly. It binds them, defines them and confers value to an otherwise transactional existence. Understanding the cultural underpinning of the overt is of deep interest to me, for life's beauty is in intricacy and nuance.

1
Culture and Counterculture

In today's world, there appears to be no other recognition in the intellectual space equal to the stature of the Nobel Prize. Shaken by the idea that he'd be remembered as a 'merchant of death', Dr Alfred Nobel willed his fortune to institute an award to distinguish people making a constructive contribution to humanity. And now, the award is invoked to signal the last of the bastions of Science and Humanities. It frames and fuels the ideals of inquiry and inspiration that hold up the values of Great Mankind.

Among the five prizes mentioned in Dr Nobel's will, one was intended for the person who, in the literary field, had produced 'the most outstanding work in an ideal direction'.

Literature, as defined by the statutes of the committee, was 'not only belles-lettres, but also other writings which, by virtue of their form and style, possess literary value'.

So, when poet-lyricist Bob Dylan was awarded a Nobel Prize in Literature in 2016 'for having created new poetic expressions within the great American song tradition', the 'literary' value of his work received polarized reactions. The literary world's response was rather tepid if not frosty. At one end, people lamented the 'come down' of the very definition of literature, and scoffed. At the other, they exhorted Dylan—a generation's voice of social protest—to not let a prize, that's founded on a wealth of armament, define him.

On prizes, then, it's been said even Mozart never won one. This reminds me of a scene in the film *Amadeus*, where Antonio Salieri, having played two pieces of music to Father Vogler—who has not recognized either—asks, 'Can you recall no melody of mine? I was the most famous composer in Europe. I wrote forty operas alone! Here, what about this one?' And he plays the first few bars of Eine Kleine Nachtmusik. Father Vogler—admiration shining in his voice—exclaims, 'Yes, I know that! I'm sorry, I didn't know you wrote that.' Antonio Salieri's cryptic yet telling dialogue, 'I didn't. That was Mozart! Wolfgang Amadeus Mozart', is a moment extraordinaire, never mind one that is more likely fictional.

So Mozart, though a practitioner of 'classical' music, frequently wrote music that was intended for the enjoyment of the common folk and was considered populist, much like Shakespeare, who, in his era, wrote for the popular audience and for profit.

LABELS

The concept of 'high art' has dominated intellectual discourse. High art is a term that includes painting, sculpture and other works that adhere to the accepted theories and practices of art. Renaissance art, classical music and opera is meant for the 'educated' and elite. 'Low art' or popular culture such as that found in contemporary mediums or mass media, like books and movies, are meant for the 'general' working-class public. So, traditionally, the hallowed art world has not considered popular culture as worthy of art. A few artists protested and rebelled against these conventions, endeavouring to break down the barricades of high art and celebrate the values of everyday life and ethos around them. The belief that there is no hierarchy of culture and that art may borrow from any source has been one of the most powerful features of popular art.

> *The established walls between the elite and common man's interests are now porous and permeable.*

This becomes even more vital when we observe that, socially and politically, we are not in the feudal age but in the era of democracy, where every voice counts. The established walls between the elite and common man's interests are now porous and permeable. And beyond the tradition of classical forms, development of industrialization, wars, technology and newer approaches, all play a role in shaping thought processes and its artistic expressions in our era.

CRITIQUE
Of course, this, in no way, implies that popular art is to be taken as is or sans the rigorous lens that is used to evaluate art forms by its most astute patrons. I don't ascribe to the point of view that critics have to be paid no heed to. Instead, to my mind, the role of a critic helps chisel an art form, which is essential in this case as well. For the role of the critic is to be a reagent between a work and its audience, and to educate and enlighten. Critique propels art to become better and cautions us against mediocrity. This is because—yes—in popular culture, there lurks the danger of something mediocre riding the wave and becoming celebrated for the not-so-right reasons. Tough standards must apply in contemporary and popular art as well. I am no advocate for audience appeasement at any cost, either. On the contrary, my belief is that there is a definite need for art for art's sake; for it to be self-indulgent, we should be able

to celebrate the 'condescension' of creators, the arrogance of artists and protect self-expression at all times. And popular-culture artists, too, must be subjected to similar erudite and searching critiques as they push the envelope. But to decide what is great art, literature or music, there has to be an element of openness, for art is an ever-evolving process of refinement. It can't be highjacked by a powerful few. It has to have space to be inclusive and nobody or no cabal should able to manipulate this.

'Popular', 'elitist' or any other kind of label should not be allowed to limit art or to sequester it by boundaries. Take for instance, the tendency to narrowly define and label certain works as folk or spiritual and put them outside the purview of literature. Should the works of Geerhardus Vos—who may be better known as a pioneer in Biblical Theology but was also an accomplished poet, producing eight volumes of poetry—be ignored? Or, for that matter, the works of Rahman Jami, who wrote eloquently on the metaphysics of mercy in the context of theology?

> *Our folk arts are replete with philosophy laced with the zeitgeist; do they not hold artistic and literary value?*

We in India, at least, should be most sensitive to this fact. Creations by Sufi mystics as well as poets such as

Surdas are branded as religious, though for me, they are no less than literature. Our folk art, be it miniature paintings, Madhubani or the works of Kabir (dohas, horis, jhoolans, manglas and baramasas) are replete with philosophy laced with the zeitgeist; do they not hold artistic and literary value? Bihari Lal 'Harit' was the first Dalit poet known as 'Jankavi' (people's poet), who brought attention to the problems of the working class. *Acchuton ka Paigambar* (Messenger of the Untouchables), a collection of his work in the rural idiom, became the voice of the poor and oppressed. By expressing in the language of the people, adopting popular speech and a simple, straightforward style, he owned their miseries and ambitions as his own. He brought in an authenticity and a contemporary social philosophy to his work. Should his stature stand diminished for not being a 'classical' poet?

BRIDGE

For some, art is an end in itself. Others believe that it's an opportunity for the true perception and criticism of the times we live in. And for some, like Swiss Dadaist sculptor Hans Ark, 'Art just is'.

There should be no hierarchy of art forms. It's not blasphemy to recite 'Do not go gentle into that good night' (Dylan Thomas) and marvel at 'Every man's conscience is vile and depraved/You cannot depend on it to be your guide when it's you who must keep it satisfied' (Bob Dylan) in the same breath, for it's not a question of which is superior—they are just diverse. Like Bob Dylan's songs breathe life into the consciousness of both, the highbrow and the ordinary folk, his fan base spans from my young daughter who 'gets' bits of 'Mr Tambourine Man', to the Ivy League literati. Culture and counterculture must coexist and so should the link of genius between both. Art and literature are ultimately created for the purpose of expressing, pontificating, mystifying, or at times, decoding life—to connect the art, the muse, the artist and the audience. Its real value to people and society is the prize—the most noble of them. And it matters little whether or not it is bestowed or accepted.

2

The Uncommon Saga of the Common Man

Driving past the Bandra–Worli Sea Link, one can't help noticing, forlorn, against the backdrop of the grey sea, R.K. Laxman's 'common man' symbolizing the silent multitude of our country. Are those whom he represents, still as silent? Or is another narrative emerging?

Joining the advertising industry during the post-liberalization period in the 1990s, one witnessed the expansion of the markets and the emergence of newer segments. One also realized—something which I was hesitant to vocalize even humbly at that point—that the profession truly required a transformation and people like me. For, a large segment of the industry whose primary reason for existence should've been their grasp of, and their ability to communicate to the target audience, they were not in sync with the ground reality. Words like 'they', 'them', 'those people' peppered the discussions. In fact, it was even strangely cool to not be associated with the middle class and the masses at large, with the undertones of them being 'downmarket'. It struck a discordant note with some of us because there is a difference between a healthy distance that helps objectivity, and a worrying disconnect.

Whilst things changed, thankfully, to a very large extent in our industry, perhaps in a broader context they ambled on. In fact, over the years, I have felt the distance—between the one who is defined as 'common man' and those who use this definition—only increase when it comes to relatability.

COMMON MAN VS AAM AADMI
Let's take a look at the portrait of the so-called common man from some vantage points. For those who live in the metros and larger cities, the common man is, willy-nilly, the one who provides the services: the milkman, the watchman, the grocery-store delivery boy, the 'bhaiyas'. He lives in some makeshift place or a 'jhuggi' (slum) or 'god knows where', arrives miraculously every morning to provide the services and disappears into the oblivion until the next day.

In the smaller cities and towns where our extended

families and older relatives reside, the common man is the one who hails from the village, where there is no electricity or running water; his wife and children rarely have distinct names and are heard of either in the context of falling ill or getting married. Apparently, his only dream is to come to the city and find employment. This is the archetype from the Premchand classics or remnants of our feudal past.

Another popular stereotype of a common man is created by cinema and media. Here exists a sense of amusement regarding this common man. In the majority of popular cinema, we often see him in a caricatured form—hell-bent on using only his dialect or regional tongue, spouting juicy abuses or risqué witticisms, possibly 'paan-chewing' and hypothetically protected from all references of the contemporary in terms of dress or behaviour. He's a suspended island and stays 'authentically regional', a misfit who entertains and amuses. After all, he is 'them', and 'they' better stay alien to the so-called progressive society. The more one spices up this character with clichés, the deeper the satisfaction of 'figuring who these people are'.

The 'urban' section of society has rarely seen a villager. The only interaction is with the reel-life version of the common man. Moreover, hardly any qualms exist in admitting that there is scant desire in them to know or engage with the real. Altered reality is a wonderful cocoon.

For a majority of the marketers, the common man

resides in PowerPoint presentations, bar graphs and Venn diagrams; in the labyrinth of psychographics, demographics, qualitative and quantitative researches; in vox populi and structured market visits and now, of course, in big data. Thankfully, in this jungle of jargons, we do have some who consider and delve deeper to understand mass consumers as respectable, distinct entities. Regrettably, they are too few and far between. Most get away with humanizing the consumer with the thoughtful 'Geeta from Gorakhpur' definition.

And yes, how can one forget the mother of them all? The common man as understood and portrayed by many politicians is an absolutely helpless animal—with barren eyes, wrinkled forehead, clothes on the verge of being tattered, asking for help. He needs nothing less than 'uddhaar' (salvation). This common man doesn't have a significant voice; he supposedly cannot understand what is right for him. He is thought of as part of a herd or *'lakhon hazaron ki bheed'* (a crowd of a hundred thousand). Of course, sometimes the 'padyatras' (foot pilgrimages) produce an inspired leap of imaginary connect with 'Shambhu from Sholapur'.

> *He's a suspended island and stays 'authentically regional', a misfit who entertains and amuses.*

The only connecting thread seems to be that of an absolute disconnect. There is little empathy, tactile sense of the struggle or sensitivity towards the largest section of our society.

AN UNDETERRED MARCH

Is it symptomatic of a society that has inequality, where people who lead are woefully distant from the ones who are led? Tulsidas wrote, *'Koi nrip hou hamau ka haani'* (Whoever be the king, it makes no difference to us). So, for far too long, the ruling class has been indifferent to and disconnected from the masses, seeking only to know of them in order to rule. The difference in food, habits, attire and language ensured that there remained a yawning gap between the ruler and the ruled.

It is the same with the bourgeoisie, which attempts to understand the market a little better so that more can be controlled and gained.

Art and cinema do have the licence of imposing fiction on fact but the problem starts when the real is used as mere prop. If *Shantaram* or *Peepli Live* become the passport, or the only defining lens to view the way 60 per cent or more of Mumbai—or, for that matter, 70 per cent of India—lives, then that is indeed quite a few degrees of separation. Reality can't be dished out in the form of crash courses. It has to be felt. It cannot be made palatable and consumable for a few.

However, as the society, across strata, starts becoming empowered, asking questions and becoming confident about their individuality, they would want things they choose, not what someone else has chosen for them. They'll demand their leadership, their products, their entertainment.

We are seeing this change in India. It has hitherto been subtle, but now it's more vigorously evident—be it the rise of local brands, leadership, or regional cinema and music. The signs of a sense of identity and a new-found confidence point towards the fact that people want to be in control of their destinies and shall resist those who talk down to them or seek to herd them. Sooner and not so later, the common man will be ready to produce his role models, leaders, marketers, filmmakers.

> *Reality can't be dished out in the form of crash courses... It cannot be made palatable and consumable for a few.*

As we journey from serfs to plebeians to the middle class, it has been encouraging to know that the currency and potency of the common man has only seen a forward trajectory.

3
Are We Free Thinkers?

Recently, while working on a new identity for an iconic brand, our discussion touched upon art historian Martin Kemp's *Christ to Coke: How Image Becomes Icon*, a book that draws some interesting comparisons between the *New Testament* Messiah and an iconic FMCG brand. Soon, however, we steered away from that course. While religions may deem to have brand codes, bringing religion into a contemporary brand narrative is a no-go zone.

But the thought kept nagging me. Do we mentally draw a line when it comes to certain areas like religion in contemporary branding? Are certain matters kept out of bounds even by some of the more 'free thinkers'? Take the tendency to narrowly define and label certain works as 'spiritual' and place them outside the purview of literature. Works by mystics and poets are branded as 'religious' even though they can well be part of the 'literary' arts.

When a Surdas writes about little Krishna insisting *'chandra khilona le hon'* (to get the moon as a toy), and a bemused Yashoda fulfils his wish with a bowl full of water so that he can play with the moon's reflection, it is an evocative depiction of the universal mother-child dynamic.

Similarly, Rahman Jami's eloquent ruminations on the metaphysics of mercy—even being in the context of theology—can only enrich any thought; as would the eight volumes of the poetic works of Geerhardus Vos, a nineteenth-century Calvinist theologian.

> *Any belief that creates distance from fellow humans is ultimately counterproductive.*

Evocative poetry and profound philosophy are found in many ideologies. Should these be readily accessed for universal enhancement and expression? Or should they be branded and ceremoniously cordoned off as 'religious'? Unfortunately, many free thinkers appear to be following the second option.

A poet's delectable insights would be less savoured, certain art less displayed, and a musical composition reservedly used, just because they have originated from a certain ideology.

BY GOD, I'M PROGRESSIVE

It is true that, for long, many of us with an artistic bone have juxtaposed theology and creativity, in the belief that the latter deals with the transgression of social norms and the former, with maintaining them. However, it is also true that many modern forms of creativity may feel limited when faced with the richness of artistic formats such as calligraphy, philosophy and iconography found in theology.

So, while it's great to be fluid in one's thinking, it doesn't imply that a deep dive into a certain ethos is resisted. An apparent link to a certain sect should not necessitate the entire content being pitched out of liberal thinking. For that would be a sure sign of a limited society. A nuanced society will be able to see, without prejudice, the inherent essence of a creative work or thought, irrespective of the context it was formed in.

So are the 'free thinkers', especially those in India, actually more dogmatic? Let's take the case of women's empowerment.

It's a clarion call and rightly so. But often it is reckoned that a working woman is an empowered, liberated woman. Do we end up shifting women from one stereotype to another? For, a woman who chooses, as a personal right and wish, to not be professionally employed, is made to fall out of the purview of the progressive/'liberated' bracket. Shouldn't true freedom and progressiveness lie in exercising an informed choice?

Are some dominant voices knowingly or unknowingly serving the cause of the polity and the marketplace? After all, contentment of any kind is counterproductive to the forces of politics and the market. So, succour provided by culture, theology and philosophy has to be decried in favour of that which is to be achieved by gratification and consumption of some kind: significance through resistance, health through expensive supplements, guidance through self-help books, beauty through artificial aids, social respect through material display, etc.

> *A truly progressive society is one where any thought or creation...can flourish for no other reason but its merit.*

Is there a deficit of humility and grace, to acknowledge that parallel narratives exist and must be engaged with, and not vociferously dismissed?

'Free thinking' in India, at some point, got entwined with affluence, elite education and stretchable societal norms. Did it also get disconnected from the masses and disengage itself from the larger narrative? It is said that the conformist lacks nuance. But, of late, is the reverse also evident?

After all, in the truly unbiased person's world, there aren't any no-go areas or pre-decided thoughts, ideologies and practices. Instead, there'd be a remarkable ability to watch a unique flower blossom on an unfamiliar ground, along with an equally deft facility to revisit familiar ground and reboot an existing stance.

LIVING IN A BRACKET

It is important to understand the space that thinkers of various hues operate in and their impact—or the lack thereof—on a larger mass consciousness. For, any belief that creates distance from fellow humans is ultimately counterproductive. The need of the hour is to examine the meanings of tags we bracket and brand ourselves in: leftists, rightists, centrists, atheists, believers, liberals, conservatives...

By probing who we think we are and how we want society to be, we can take cognizance of the fact that a truly progressive society is one where any thought or creation, irrespective of its origin and genesis, can flourish for no other reason but its merit.

4
Why Such Violentainment?

I totally look forward to the list of must-watch TV shows, web series, films and gaming, and simultaneously, at times, venture into the waters of GECs (General Entertainment Channels). However, browsing through the portals of entertainment, one striking aspect which seems pervasive, is an ungainly amount of programming which is drawing from the basics of animalistic behaviour: unabashed violence, sex, mutilation, gore and more.

Come to think of it, I don't think it'd be fair to call it animalistic. In fact, animal behaviour seems to have the justification and logic of survival. One cannot ascribe vilifying labels like 'sadistic lion', 'spiteful giraffe', 'hurtful rabbit'—that's only in their human depiction. The animal world is, by far, nonchalant. They seldom kill out of sheer spite or indulge in studied cruelty and torture.

So, what is the reason behind such depictions? Why are the so-called period dramas (medieval or prehistoric) and the crop of crime, horror and 'serial killer' shows—many artistically done, with good production values but a shocking dose of gruesome violence and body count—finding so much popularity?

One view is that violence—direct and indirect—has been a part of the human DNA. Killing, loot, plunder, wars and civil strife have existed since time immemorial, often as a show of strength. But as civilizations evolved, a shift away from the barbaric tendencies and towards more non-violent societies has been at play. In fact, statistics show that violence in the last five decades has been at an all-time low. A significant fall in world wars, capital and corporal punishment, homicides—all the data show downward trends, when compared to previous centuries. Terrorism is, of course, the anomaly, but many academics and statisticians look at its impact, clinically, as 'low death-high publicity' phenomena.

In this seemingly more evolved society, where even smacking your own child is frowned upon and a concerted effort to weed out forms of force is afoot, it's interesting to see that the space which violence acquired in our natural lives, is shifting into the virtual world—a domain which we consciously create and have full control over. There are no unchained forces of nature in the reckoning here; it's all the invention of the human mind where we have all the tools of imagination to create something wonderful.

So, the questions come storming into the head: Instead of creating something uplifting and inspiring, why is there an overarching appeasement to the basal, and a conscious creation of delinquencies, angst, slaughter and carnage, to such a bloated degree? What is the appeal of this violent programming, where one struggles to spot human goodness—where the majority of characters are dark and negative; where sunshine is a rare commodity?

> *It seems that deep down, humans still want a manifestation of their basic physicality.*

'IF IT BLEEDS, IT LEADS'

In the journalistic world, to catch instant attention, there may be an adherence to 'if it bleeds, it leads', but in the mass entertainment world, what is the basic appeal? Which buttons are being pressed? Confronting violence in our real lives and also continuing to seek stimulated violence and darker human emotions in the reel world is intriguing.

To delve deeper into the consumption of so much

'violentainment' as it were, we need to examine whether civilized society is an acquired thought; whether there is something unnatural about civilization itself. It seems that deep down, humans still want a manifestation of their basic physicality. If I remember correctly, the cult film *Fight Club*, too, touched upon this premise.

A Coliseum bull fight, homegrown traditions of cock fight and many other versions of bloodied sport have found considerable space in our modern world. Aside from the glorification of the spirit of human effort that sport embodies, physicality and brutality are manifest in specific contact sports like wrestling and boxing. Yet they are cheered and spurred, albeit under the sanitized cloak of healthy competition.

Is it that, on one hand, we strive for civilized behaviour and do succeed in significant terms, but on the other, it's largely posturing and we hanker for a constant dose of venting—violently? And this 'balancing out' persists?

Increasingly, it doesn't look quite so subconsciously benign. There is now conscious consumption of violence.

So, whilst in the real world—forget fist cuffs—even verbal abuse is frowned upon, the online and gaming world belies all the moralistic coding and engages millions with its pitiless and vicious content. In this virtual world, the body and its primal compunctions are out of the fray. It's now the mind that requires a dose of violence. Successful new content has vampires, zombies, bone collectors, devious politicians, criminals, sharpshooters and more.

VIOLENCE IS NOT NEW; ACCEPTANCE IS

Interestingly, there is a clever use of the licence of the ancient and medieval world setting and time, to depict these blood-gore-sex sagas and the smart use of 'we are just depicting the barbaric world that was'. One of my pet theories at one point was that when, as a society, we occasionally consume dark content, there's a counterpoint at play: When one encounters the worst of society, the ability to appreciate the mediocrity of your personal world becomes easier.

> *There have been proponents of 'aesthetic murder' as well; deeming it in some cases, a kind of artistry.*

That aside, whilst the depiction of forced sex, violence and crime is not new and was a part of our lives, perhaps the mainstream acceptance of it in our world today, is. I recall, whilst growing up in north India, the crime and gore in regional publications like *Manohar Kahani* or *Satyakatha* were not considered respectable, and below the standards of the intellectually-aware, well-read and well-educated class. But even this seems redundant in the face of the 'mainstreaming and sheer popularity' of vicarious violence-themed fare.

On a more academic level, the 'aesthetic of violence' in art, theatre, literature or film has been discussed for centuries. From the Greek tragedies to the works of Quentin Tarantino, violence has got its place in the sun as a form of expressive art. And I have no qualms in admitting that I've been captivated too; for violence, at times, is presented in such a visually stunning manner and with such elegant agility, that it does shock and awe. There have been proponents of 'aesthetic murder' as well, deeming it in some cases, a kind of artistry. Lacing this with a more philosophical lattice: Violence being played out as a spectacle—with others acting and enduring our innermost fears—has often thought to serve as a catharsis.

However, it's also true that what goes on in the theatre of our mind or on the actual screen in our home—in fantasies—and how it plays out in real life, are all connected, however tenuously.

Thankfully, the redeeming aspect of humanity is that we have minds that can question, debate and attempt to understand conflicting phenomenon.

So, before generalizing 'refinement' as a borrowed thought, a utopian concept that weighs light in the context of a more primal force, let's not forget that the need for civilization, too, has come about organically. Compassion, sensitivity and camaraderie are as intrinsic to, and as much a part of, the human nature as feral behaviour. What we need to strive for is to fan the former and weed out the latter.

This is easier said than done, for till injustice and inequality remain and grow, so would the need to vent and for the visceral to ignite. As we ruminate over this phenomenon, let's keep trying to make more room for the Poetry of Life.

5

Social Walls: Demolish Convenient Windows for the Real View

India, alongside much of the world, seems to be in a state of alarm about 'people like that' who are propelling political and social change. The disruption of the old social order seems to have created, for many, a 'tyranny of the masses', a sudden pervasiveness of 'inferiors'—apparently an intellectually, socially, culturally deficient lot; conservative; brash; and lacking in the upper-class lingua franca. Confusion prevails in trying to define this phenomenon though, much like with the definition of the 'common man' (as discussed in an earlier chapter in this book). Whilst the term 'common man' has expansive prevalence in India—with entities across the continuum brandishing it like a weapon—who exactly is the 'saadharan aadmi' or 'aam aurat'—the 'aam vyakti' (the ordinary man or common woman—the common person)? Those barely above the shameful poverty line, the 'middle class', the powerless, the ones moving up the ladder, all of these—or someone altogether different? Over the years, I have felt the distance, between those defined as the common person and those who use this definition, only increase when it comes to being able to genuinely relate.

There is a historical backdrop to the sudden clashes/disruptions that we see coming from the common man or masses. For centuries, our ruling class was not connected to the masses. In that scenario, the real was often used as a mere prop. If *Slumdog Millionaire* or *Peepli Live* become the passport or the defining lens to view how much of India lives in slums or hinterlands, then that is indeed quite a few degrees of separation. However, to bracket this purely as 'elites' clashing with 'commoners', would be simplistic.

> *For centuries, our ruling class was not connected to the masses...the real was often used as a mere prop.*

LITTLE EXPOSURE LEADS TO UNEASE

Reality has to be felt raw. It cannot be made palatable for a few. At one of the recent literature festivals I attended, many were lamenting the loss of poetry and the emergence of a lewd lexicon in the songs of our contemporary popular culture. A Bollywood song like 'Munni Badnaam Hui' makes the genteel uneasy. But the fact is that the origin of this song can be traced back to 'Launda Badnaam Hua', a Bhojpuri song which was sung in small 'nautankis' (dramas) for scores of years before the reel version happened.

The unease comes from having had little exposure to 'those' people, 'that' kind of living. Some of us have led a culturally shielded life, where every linguistic morsel was carefully chosen and placed tastefully on our seasoned palate. Music, art and poetry were inculcated and a wall existed between the elite and the rest. The food, music, clothing and sensibilities of both were at complete odds.

But there also exists a parallel world, surviving with a simmering sensibility. After all, finesse is not the prerogative of a subset of society. A certain dialect, which on the face of it, seems crass to our preconditioned accent, could actually be sophisticated in thought. I recall being struck with the intricacy of intent when I read about an African tribe that has a song and prayer to ask for the forgiveness and bless the soul of the animal after a hunt. Or take the simple Pahadi song 'Chappal Ke Lacha Yasa', where a woman complains to her husband: 'What kind of a slipper have you got me, which does not make a sound of "phat phat" when I walk?' This has allure, nuance and onomatopoeia.

CONVENIENT WINDOWS, SANITIZED VISIONS

Perhaps, we have lost the appetite, the courage and the honesty to see the larger reality, and instead, have created cozy versions and convenient windows through which we can peek at a sanitized version of the real—be it films, theatre, books, or travel. An interesting example is the proverbial 'Ramu kaka' figure in our films—the trusted 'man-nanny' of the elite world. This 'reel' stereotype was taken for 'real', without realizing that we knew little about Ramu kaka's life's truths, his reality, his surname, the food he enjoyed or the language he spoke in his village? We simply used a narrow media lens to observe a much broader reality.

However, media is a two-way traffic. As one lot peeked into a larger culture, the larger culture, too, stared back, consumed and tailored the codes of the other side. The signs are telling: International foods like pasta and soup are now mass-marketed; 'niche' products of art, music, clothing and travel are now consumed by a larger section of society too. The media's dark era, where luxury, opulence and creature comforts resided in tales that were far from the grasp of the multitude, and democracy was just a term, has given way to more openness.

> *For, at times, the truth is in between two sharp notes... The substance is not in the 'or.' It's in the 'and'.*

Sometimes, the sacred also becomes placid. A '-cracy', '-ism' or philosophical belief can find itself locked in a language capsule. It is only when the capsule breaks and is ingested by an ecosystem, does it become a felt reality.

Thankfully, that is what is happening to 'democracy' now. The walls are more permeable than ever before. Social and status mobility is a highway now, not a narrow one-way street. And this is not easy to come to terms with.

The resistance to change, by large sections of the beneficiaries of the older order, is palpable. Often, the impending change is stated with warnings of impending doom. But we have to be ready to shake ourselves out of our comfort zones and realize that a status quo is never the answer. The choice—to not feel victimized by change, but contribute and give direction to it—will need to be made.

Change should also not imply throwing the baby out with the bathwater. There are immensely far-sighted intellectuals in our country, who can clearly see the contemporary picture. Their views should be solicited, for one can't always make it about black or white, or be forced to decide once and for all. Us versus them; class versus mass; sane versus the 'mindlessly' angry; liberals versus conservatives; ethnicity versus multiculturalism; folks versus trolls; patriotism versus nationalism; futurists versus navel gazers; globalization versus localization—we simply have to find an equilibrium. For, at times, the truth is in between two sharp notes—a 'teevra madhyam' (a sharp middle), as one would call it in Indian classical music. The substance is not in the 'or'. It's in the 'and'.

6

Post-truth: The Fiction About Fact

Frequent flare-ups, especially in the world of cinema, seem to be garnering a lot of attention. Controversies have been multiple and there seems to be a face-off between certain public sentiments and popular culture. Many contend it's a phenomenon unique to the times we live in. This is not just limited to India but many parts of the world, which have woken up to various kinds of issues. Is there something unprecedented going on or are we suddenly reacting to sentiments that were 'non-issues' earlier?

This takes me back to the closing debate on 'post-truth' at the Jaipur Literature Festival in 2017. While many in the audience may have been familiar with the term 'post-truth', the understanding of it differed. So what is this 'post-truth' era—a phrase that is being liberally used to brand the public and socio-political environment?

The general premise of post-truth seems to be that emotions and beliefs have become more important and facts have taken a back seat. My contention is slightly different: Haven't belief and emotion always been more powerful than reality? They have inspired, created, propelled, held strong—be it in institutions or social movements. They have also made the impossible, possible, in the face of facts and figures that stated the odds and the given order: A double amputee scaling Everest; Guru Gobind Singh's stirring *'sava lakh se ek ladaun'* (one Sikh against 1.25 lakh enemies), which tapped into self-pride; or the emotional belief of *'paradheen sapne hun sukh nahin'* (there is no happiness under subjugation), which drove a colonized nation to overthrow a seemingly reformist imperial rule.

Of course, the argument of how extreme or negative emotions have led to transgressions, abound as well. But to disdainfully portray 'emotions and beliefs' taking precedence as a recent phenomenon and as a lesser element of a societal fabric, reeks of an approach sans any nuance.

My attempt is to broaden the frame, for which a little more sensitivity and acceptance needs to come into play. We need to examine the lenses and filters we apply and our biases that have developed over several years—especially the intelligentsia's.

People who were beneficiaries of the progress and development of society seem to have let the gap widen. Decisions taken on behalf of society were often on the premise that 'we know', though on ground, there was a growing disconnect.

Good thinking and the right intent apart, there were numerous issues of the masses that were swept under the carpet or brushed aside in a somewhat condescending 'these people do not know what's good for them' manner. For years, this continued and the common man surrendered to the decisions made on his or her behalf. Sure, the people were offered a democratic setup, but despite casting the ballot, there was, at best, limited empowerment; for, very soon, their so-called representatives donned the seat vacated by the 'rulers' and the masses continued to live under the old shadow of being reigned over, not truly represented. Not that currently the ideal meaning and power of democracy is in play either, for people still get manipulated. But a certain awareness and expression is seeping in, albeit in an unusual manner.

This is so, because issues were latent in the hearts and minds of people. There was pent-up and bottled emotion, which is now finding its way out. The many issues, especially with cinema today, are not because it is a 'soft target' but because it is a dominant force in the prevalent discourse. The very scale of cinema and its audio-visual power has the ability to change a narrative forever in the public consciousness.

Is cinema is obliged to shoulder more responsibility? Well, for starters, let's recognize that all alternate narratives have been subsumed in cinema. The sheer power of the audio-visual medium and its glaring presence hardly left any room for the humbler narratives—folk and tribal music, regional theatre, poetry and other such art forms—many of which found it difficult to survive in the face of a potent force and sought shelter in a diluted form, in the all-pervasive realm of cinema, especially in India. For example, it may be surprising for many across the world that we don't have a self-sufficient parallel music industry. It has long been in the service of celluloid. Rarely did cinema take cognizance of the fact that its pervasiveness has choked—not nurtured or amplified—gentler artistic murmurs, which were a small but relatable means of public expression. On the other hand, a large section of cinema gradually began losing its sensitivity. Rather than art, it was mainly the commerce of cinema that is celebrated. This corroded the very basis on which it called for special, softer treatment. Borrowing from culture and the lives of people, sans a modicum of responsibility, cinema may now find it difficult to have a free emotional hall pass to sheer profit.

> *The people were offered a democratic setup, but despite casting the ballot, there was, at best, limited empowerment.*

Today, people are exposed to information and if they want to disagree with a viewpoint, they express it in various ways. Media and connectivity have also given voice and confidence to people who thought they were fighting a battle in a suspended world of their own. However, pinning all this on social media and covert digital cells, or narrowing it to the ruling party and people in power, will be myopic. Something organic is at play, too; for there is social media and there is social change.

Call or react to it by any name, change there is. Rather than lament, we need to hear, acknowledge and address it. The issues being raised should not once again be dismissed as the cultural issues of the cattle class or politically motivated, and have their shortcomings flung on their faces or branded as lies. We should dig deep to understand and question that if a lie has resonated, is it because it reflects a certain truth? It's critical that a culturally acceptable and cohesive platform to table these issues be created by reaching out and listening. Some issues may be found to be frivolous as expected, and some others, unexpectedly logical and real. Violence needs to be condemned absolutely, but the chapter doesn't close there. The reasons behind the tipping point ought to be identified. People should be encouraged to bring forth issues rather than meted a dismissal; in turn, generating a feeling that the only way to be heard is a street agitation, or an 'andolan'.

We need a more compassionate society that can acknowledge its lapses and come to terms with having to mend fences, rather than create more 'us versus them' narratives. The ones exposed to a more global worldview should be open to dialogue with those with a varied logic and thought and those who didn't have the same opportunities that the privileged had. As far as truth goes, we must acknowledge that different perspectives will produce different views or interpretations. But this may be the silver lining in this world of hyper-connectivity, wherein we can see these perspectives, these shafts of light falling from different directions. They will only make the object clearer.

> *Call or react to it by any name, change there is. Rather than lament, we need to hear, acknowledge and address it.*

To go into a shell or be swept up in change, is perhaps easier; it is more difficult to steer to a direction where the light of hope resides.

Personally, I would strive for the latter. It's not the time to rail against 'the other' and lament about post-truth; it's time to acknowledge the current, larger reality and make a new beginning.

7

Surrogacy Saga: Looking for a Silver Lining

Surrogacy has given a ray of hope to many, bringing the patter of tiny feet to childless couples well past the expiry date of their hopes. Same-sex couples and singles have access to a tool that allows them to realise an unfulfilled dream. With this view of surrogacy, I heard a friend recount how, often during the procedure, two or more embryos are planted in two women, and if the pregnancy occurs in more than one, the other is made to abort. The physical pain is treatable; the psychological turmoil, perhaps, not as easily. A newborn in the arms of ecstatic parents often blurs the memory of the path taken. The ends justify the means. Or do they?

The proposed Surrogacy (Regulation) Bill, 2016, to regulate commercial surrogacy has raked up many sentiments. Surrogacy is a complex issue. Let's explore it from different vantage points. One, of the person desperate to have a child: The yearning could be biological—the social pressures of 'kul/vansh' (lineage), or the need to see one's own flesh and blood; the inability to produce a child is indeed devastating. And the second, from that of the surrogates: Their motives range from being part of a noble cause to financial empowerment; there are also tales of coercion and exploitation.

SOCIETY SANS SURROGACY

Let's reflect on the situation from a few decades ago, when surrogacy was largely absent. What kind of a society was this absence nudging us towards? Many would recount stories of couples being under tremendous pressure—divorces, remarriages and other desperate measures—to have a child. But a silver lining was emerging. The boundaries of norms were being pushed. It compelled people to accept and overcome certain situations, to open their hearts, to rise above circumstances.

> *The definition of a woman was being broadened to a person with various dimensions and not just a child-producing machine.*

Statistically, these cases may have been few, but a change was brewing and will slowly face a trickle-down effect in society. It was asking questions of narrow-minded people: Why can't you love your wife and/or your daughter-in-law, even if she can't bear a child? Why is it the only factor that defines them?

The definition of a woman was being broadened to a person with various dimensions and not just a child-producing or 'vansh-vriddhi' (carrying forward the generation) machine. It encouraged couples—heterosexual and homosexual—to view their relationships as living up to the vow of being together through thick and thin, finding completeness in one another, not divorcing or remarrying, but staying together despite the pressures nature or society placed on them to procreate.

It awakened a better belief: Adopting was an option. Every couple that chose adoption was signalling that a woman is more than a child-bearer and in cases of male infertility, that he was a man, irrespective of his sperm count. That despite genetic background, by nurturing, embedding values and kindling love, one could create a beautiful bond for life—a bond that endures beyond the biological. It was challenging caste, creed and religion, and breaking barriers—one adoptive family at a time. The absence of surrogacy was propelling society in a more humane and constructive direction.

Surrogacy, in many ways, underscores the belief that only biological offspring are worthy of complete parental commitment and love. Paid surrogacy takes a society backwards. Now, one doesn't have to change a narrow mindset, overcome base instincts or expand one's thinking because science and commerce can change individual reality. In many cases, it also gives leeway to conformist patriarchal setups that were slowly accepting girls as inheritors, by providing them with an easy way to have male heirs.

> *Surrogacy can be an option when done with genuine empathy and responsibility.*

GENUINE EMPATHY

Irrespective of patriarchal setups, and respecting individual choice, surrogacy can be an option when done with genuine empathy and responsibility, where a woman, informed of all aspects (physical, mental, emotional) of being a surrogate, makes a considered, personal decision, without any coercion or ulterior motive. If it is about two people who can look each other in the eye and say, 'This is the truth we share', I am all for it. If it's about money and power, about being able to exploit and use the weak, about the greed to propagate one's genes getting the better of human emotions, and about shortcuts, then it needs to be examined.

When an overwhelming majority of surrogates are from the vulnerable sections of society, something is not right. It is not right when it's a 'third party contract', from which the intermediaries profit. Something is amiss when, in most cases, the surrogate and the intended parents don't even know each other. Something is amiss when it's a class divide—you rarely see a more privileged woman as a surrogate for a less economically privileged woman. Something is not right when human life is reduced to a financial transaction.

Families today are created in many different ways, but we still need to find answers to certain issues. For example, many women undergoing IVF (in vitro fertilization) are distressed about it being a degrading process—having their body prodded and pumped with hormonal cocktails that can be life-threatening—but they go through it to have their own biological child. How, then, must it be for a commercial surrogate—a woman and a human being—to undergo a similar procedure, not for emotional or biological fulfilment, but for money? Is 'financial gains for the family of the surrogate and her children' a sound argument, or should there be better ways to economically empower women?

What about the rights of the child? There's more than enough evidence to show how harrowing it is for a newborn to be separated from its birth mother. This occurrence, in cases of accidents or abandonments, is bad enough, but how right is it when done deliberately, for the child has not entered into any 'contract' like that between the biological parents and the surrogate?

What happens in cases like that of one of a pair of twins, a baby called Gammy, born to a Thai surrogate, who was abandoned by his biological parents from Australia as he had Down Syndrome; or an almost identical case where a baby boy born to an Indian surrogate, was left behind by his biological parents, who flew back with his twin sister, citing they could afford only one child? Can we turn a blind eye and sweep things under the carpet by claiming that the ends justify the means?

The answers to some of these questions can, at times, be offered by a legal framework, but not always. Sometimes, only our conscience has the answers. Thinking responsibly for all concerned and taking action to plug the loopholes in the system is progressive, not regressive. Any practice or proposed law should be examined from the lens of intent, efficacy and having taken into account the issues of all sections of society. Every voice needs to be heard and, if legitimate, catered to. Think, feel, debate and introspect. Then make informed, sensitive choices.

SECTION 2

Thinking Unplugged

One can say that the mind is in the thought or that the thought is in the mind. For me, thought and mind are not separate; they exist as one unitary moment.

The question to grapple with is: Do we have any control at all over our thoughts, or do they randomly appear on the canvas of our mind? The answer to that is subjective but one aspect which we can most agree on is that we can choose the kind of fodder to give our mind to chew on. The richer and more complex that is, the finer will be the thought.

In my experience, the randomness of thought is natural, but steering them in a desired direction is learnt. We need both—spontaneity and purpose.

8

Material Branding of the Abstract: Real Art, Packaged Products and the Thin Line

In a conversation with a friend's young son a couple of days ago, the topic of 'marketing' came up. Having seen him grow up as a talented musician, I was intrigued to hear him discuss the nuances of promotion and publicity.

It got me thinking more deeply about whether there was any real difference between 'products' and 'products of art', that is, artistic products.

Creative satisfaction used to be an exclusive prerogative of the practitioners of 'pure art'. Today, we can see people deriving creative satisfaction from varied activities. In fact, in our modern world, 'creativity' is now a very loosely used term. Its realm has been stretched from all ends and many have stepped in and over the borderlines.

Business has found an enviable space in artistic solutions. One can well imagine a visual of currency notes floating in slow motion with an intricate classical music symphony playing in the background. The space of 'pure art', 'pure intellect', 'pure talent', or 'pure anything', that needed to be prioritized over money, is no more sacred.

Of course, there has always been commissioned art—be it Michelangelo's magnificent work for the Sistine Chapel commissioned by the Pope, or classical ragas composed for visiting dignitaries at a king's palace. But perhaps the fusion of art and commerce is even more pronounced—and more seamless—in our times.

Today's artists are no more associated with the suffering, intrinsic pain and textured plight of life like one associated with Vincent van Gogh, Franz Kafka, Suryakant Tripathi 'Nirala' or Gajanan Muktibodh. Today, the romantic notion of art is confined to mannerism and appearance of a certain kind, and under no circumstance do we see money taking the back seat.

We have—at least for the short term—successfully created an ecosystem where professions and industries like research labs and manufacturing units now access creativity freely. In fact, we hear words like 'brainstorming', 'innovation', 'spark' and 'paradigm shift' in industries—the very castles of conformity where you rarely heard these words in the past.

And why not? Our world is blurring the lines and accessing the compartments where creativity and art forms once resided exclusively.

ARTISTIC PRODUCTS

I have mentioned the words 'artistic products' earlier. We have come to accept that art necessarily doesn't have to be an enemy of money. And one can achieve commercial success while also achieving artistic excellence, simultaneously. This, in turn, has evolved a new reality where marketing of art has become an art in itself.

> 'Artistic product' is not an oxymoron. It's a reality of our world today.

We are now admiring the business strategies of selling artistic products such as films and music as well as paintings and books. I often meet creative people today who not only have a creative idea but also have a clear marketing strategy for their creation. Books are thought of with a cover design in mind and film concepts are thought of with the sponsorships and brand affiliations it may attract. So, yes, 'artistic product' is not an oxymoron. It's a reality of our world today.

Post the shift in the early nineteenth century when objectivity was applied to art, to the impressionist's view of art being pure self-expression, many argue that this has led to the slipping of the standards of art—for, self-expression (another loosely used term) has diluted the various forms of art to allow an 'anything goes' aspect.

Many are disappointed with the loss of romance in art. The belief that creativity and forms of art are not supposed to be a commodity—that art is a musing, a rumination on the human condition, an embodiment of the zeitgeist—doesn't seem to connect with ground reality. And despite being in the thick of this new reality, there's a belief that one should not hide one's longing for what is lost—or is, at least, rapidly disappearing.

People call this the democratization of, and end of elitism in, art. But for me, the bigger truth is economic and the underlying laziness of the mind, which goes hand in hand with the world of instant gratification. Though commercial aspects need not be anathema to artists, some lines may irreversibly be blurred and a lot will be lost when business is the intent and creation a byproduct.

EASY CREATIVITY

There is little denying that we are now living in a mutable society. So, what does the future of artistic products look like? Today's so-called artistic products seem to be living off the equity of real art—the genuine art in which generations have invested their time, suffering, hard work, sacrifices, instinct and unpredictability.

We will get gradually bored and dissatisfied with the current form of easy creativity and will seek the real deal. But this time, the difference would be in the way we consume it.

Real pain, real sacrifice and real suffering would become an industry itself. You would seek real art but would want a packaged product.

> *Some lines may irreversibly be blurred and a lot will be lost when business is the intent and creation a byproduct.*

Suffering art. Painful art. It is almost like the way we consume spirituality in packaged form today—the material branding of the abstract.

For now, it is the art of commercialization which seems to be the dominant force of the times.

9

Creativity in Adversity

Being a poet at heart and an advertising person by vocation, at times, I tend to see creation in two distinct compartments: self-expression and business-related.

When creation is for self-expression, it is innate, entirely spontaneous. There is little choice; one can't help but create. It's a natural state and the commerce of it, if any, is just a byproduct.

I see this joy of creation, for self-expression, taking front seat once again. For a while now, the atmosphere prevailing in our society has been conducive for art and commerce to walk far too closely—with, in fact, the latter leading. There were too many market considerations: the booming economy, the growth of new consumer segments, the researches and forecasting of what the consumer wants and will want, and the kind of art that would be lucrative to create, buy or invest in. These were the driving forces. Creativity and its expression was becoming made-to-order.

This was not surprising, for when markets are growing at breakneck speed, the concentration turns towards maximum output at minimum input. In fact, the input is of diminutive value. Society is content with the ostensible beauty of art; its inherent thought and angst perhaps are not completely relatable. So, natural and raw expressions take a back seat and a forced creation cycle comes into play. However, when societies go through major crises like the global economic slowdown, terror attacks (such as one that took place in Mumbai in 2008) or the systemic failure of socio-political structures, I strongly feel creativity revisits its spontaneous state. The overwhelming emotion lets creativity follow a natural course which is not directed as much by market considerations. Sure, art forms and cultural life are intrinsic to the social edifice and truly flourish when there is financial stability. However, often

> *Human creativity has indeed peaked between a crumbling past and a rising future.*

when art's economic dimension is diminished, it turns into a powerful tool for self and social expression.

In any case, societal conflict and harsh economic circumstances have been conducive for varied art forms to emerge and thrive, be it writing, art, music or newer forms. The angst, insecurity and vulnerability of a generation are tipping points for inspired thought and expression, be it as a result of, or precursor to, societal upheaval.

When a collective sense of injustice and anger takes over from mere individual hedonism, and social consciousness and defiant energy gets an edge, it reflects in creative expression. The Great Depression of the 1930s in the US or the Renaissance in Europe were defining periods for artistic imagination and creative expression. Difficult times in the '70s and '80s defined hip-hop globally and music bands with their sharp lyrics became part of the youth's demands. It's fascinating to note how, in 2001, during the economic crisis in Argentina, spray-painted stencil art was frugally used to make 'spontaneous murals' by anonymous artists using X-rays found in hospital trash. Protests, neighbourhood demonstrations and stencil street art were all tied together. Human creativity has indeed peaked between a crumbling past and a rising future.

Additionally, I believe that there will be enormous public participation during such difficult times. All those who feel the need for self-expression—amateur or otherwise—shall find a platform and audience, however limited. Be it through blogs or other self- and community-created forums, art would increasingly become public and accessible. Creativity is not going to be the domain of a few.

There may be efforts to redefine and collectively create 'heroes'—not on the silver screen but off it. There would be an increased need for 'rooted in life' figures who personify the angst and display the ability to overcome. We might witness an emergence, in thought and reality, of new kind of role models who would define the essence of society at this juncture.

I also see, for the duration of such times, our creation becoming more genuine, more rooted. Pure entertainment could be seen as frivolous in light of what has impacted us as a country. Meaningfulness and creativity will marry and become a potent and real force. Creativity will find a direction. Agreed, that art and creative pursuits have been consumed as a relief factor or as light escapism in trying circumstances. But I believe they will be viewed more consciously and responsibly than ever before. The suspension of thinking and the distancing from a larger truth will not be as extensive.

> *Undefined and dithering mores allow space for randomness of ideas, and sometimes the randomness is beautiful.*

In today's date, people want to face the reality. There is a more thought-provoking approach, a genuine desire to get a more idealistic grip and understand what's happening around us. Many may not have that approach, but certainly, there shall be added takers for a more profound, gritty and socially conscientious creativity.

However, looking from another perspective, the above aspect, in a way, will also put a break on unbridled creativity. I say this because when creativity finds reason and is anchored in the social truth, what may happen is that the radical and totally out-of-the-box ideas not conforming to this reality, can get rejected.

Tragic national or international happenings will provide a common ethical filter and an intellectual anchor to the society whose principles and stance may have got muddled. Grappling with materialism, a new kind of balance is sought. Undefined and dithering mores allow space for randomness of ideas, and sometimes the randomness is beautiful. But when a balance is found—like it seems now, despite its pluses—it may, in a sense, be limiting. For when society views things from a single vantage point, the fluidity of a thought process that is not in sync with it, is impacted. Creativity thrives in some chaos.

Stripped down to a personal level, I genuinely feel that there should be a deep change in relatively minor individual aspects. I hope that apart from all the significant and society-altering creative expressions, we also find the time to pause and appreciate the small expressions around us.

Most of all, I hope that creativity and the arts will always find lovers, believers and patrons, and not mere consumers.

10
Ideas: The Liminal Space

Often this question is posed at creative people in my field: 'How do you come up with ideas?'

Personally speaking, I don't think I have ever come up with an idea. As far as I remember, ideas have always come to me. For me, they are free floating bodies in the ether space and one's sensibilities are like a receiver—sharper the receiver, easier it is for the ideas to get attracted.

In a very definite and defined state, new thoughts have rarely emerged; if I clearly know what I want, it's too focused and too uninspiring for originality to surface. It is the 'liminal' space—literally being on the sensory threshold—which is often responsible for ideas. It's a frustrating place to be in because it's not tethered or defined, but at the same time it's a very idea-friendly state.

Dabbling in varied fields like poetry, advertising, cinema, social issues and music impels me to explore the nuances of varied structures and forms.

As a creative person, it becomes important to develop one's sensibilities and work on the craft because ideas have to be expressed in varied forms—be it art, writing, music or other forms. A brilliant idea cannot shine if it's not backed by exceptional craft. It's a shame when many great ideas fade away without getting their due, because they lacked good execution.

> *A wire cannot say, 'I am electricity'; it simply carries it. Similarly, all one can do is to become a worthy medium for good ideas...*

I'm a bit averse to looking too hard for an idea. It's more of letting the task soak in, letting it filter into the subconscious mind. In Indian ethos, this is called 'nimit'— you are just a medium. And a medium should never take itself too seriously. A wire cannot say, 'I am electricity'; it simply carries it. Similarly, all one can do is to become a worthy medium for good ideas and to become one, it helps to be a student of life. I try to be absorbed in life, without any biases, as ideas are source-agnostic. Sure, one has a certain perspective and some filters are bound to exist, but I try to be in the moment and soak it all in, sans preconceptions. Ideas, after all, emanate from the subconscious; that's the processor in our system. We need to make available, all kinds of experiences and thoughts as 'material'. Ideas are the culmination, and the prep work is being done all the time, subliminally.

The one time I work consciously is whilst reading the brief or discussing the task. I get as much information as possible, on all aspects that open the mind and flood it with details. Post that, I let myself be. The mind keeps on ticking and gradually thoughts start forming.

Rigour doesn't necessarily make one a better ideator, but it does a very important thing—it sharpens the understanding and alertness towards recognizing a great idea. One learns to differentiate between real ideas and those that posture as one.

A confession: I have a special corner in my heart for deadlines because I perform best when racing against time. Creative people often procrastinate and it helps to be whipped into shape by time.

11
Asian Creativity: Indefinable, Limitless

Often, on international forums I am asked: 'What can Asia teach the world about creativity?'

It'd be very presumptuous to say what Asia can 'teach'; let's simply explore what stands out as unique about Asia and the kind of work—literary or artistic—that it produces.

At this juncture of time, to my mind, there is much uniformity, a sort of a pattern that the developed Western world has settled into. Be that of language, palate, social structures and so on, the Western narrative seems a bit fatigued.

Asia, on the other hand, has very fresh imagery: The vibrancy, the pulsating sense of life on the move, the sheer diversity. Asia continues to confound. There is a lot of order and a set sensibility that may appear in parts of Asia, e.g., Japan or Singapore. But for most part, what bursts forth is the utter complexity. The languages, landscapes, culture, food, religions, gender dynamics—all are at different stages across Asia and most often than not, different even in the same place. There is a coexistence of contradictions. Parts of Asia are hi-tech; parts of it look stuck in time. Newer thoughts are accepted without ancient wisdoms being altered. There is a blurring of lines, a certain comfort with chaos. This may be truer of Asian pockets like India or parts of South East Asia, but it is a broad stroke you can paint Asia with.

Where Asia scores is that, in large parts, it is already spontaneously practising the social buzzword, 'transculturalism', where there is a little bit of mine, a little bit of yours and a third, completely new form of culture, that is emerging as a hybrid of the two.

This ease with things changing, and yet not panicking about letting go, stems from the philosophical beliefs of Buddhism, Hinduism or other ancient Eastern philosophies, which profess that the concept of time is cyclical—the coexistence of the past, present and future.

This is fertile ground for both the new and the old. Introducing something new doesn't necessarily mean weeding out the old—be it a thought, concept or product. There is space for extremes.

The ability to adapt has resulted in a richer sensibility. There has been low resistance to influences, and Western thought and practice have been interpreted and integrated in a whole new manner. The theory of reincarnation, of the existence of an internal soul which continues to exist by just changing the external garb is perhaps reflective in Asia's consciousness. The ability to retain the core and change the paraphernalia is immense. In our brand and communication context, when we talk of a global idea, this understanding is perhaps useful. The approach that a brand/idea can take various forms whilst remaining true to its core, will perhaps find more acceptance in Asia.

> *The ability to retain the core and change the paraphernalia is immense.*

I'd also like to touch upon another Asian attribute—profoundness. Given that the cultures are ancient and there is a distinct oral tradition, the wisdom has soaked into daily life. The ability to make profound statements in a simple manner and the apparent ease with which higher philosophies of life are part of everyday conversations is unique to Asia.

How a product, fulfilling a very basic function, could be elevated into something meaningful is perhaps a learning. People here consume emotions and feelings more than mere material consumption. The ability to consume and yet not get consumed by it, is distinctive. The more developed, economically saturated societies where material consumption has peaked, where greed is not considered so good anymore, can perhaps take from Asia the ability to see beyond pure consumption and actively look for recreating a value system and not just products.

Asia is a fabric that can easily change every inch of its warp and weft. Its ability to absorb—to not just assimilate but celebrate differences—is what makes Asian creativity so indefinable and so limitless.

12

The New Frontier: Creativity in the Changing Times

John Lennon wouldn't have imagined that geophysical barriers would be dissolving thus. Products and brands today reach potential consumers the world over, instantaneously. We can find any metadata, anywhere, any time, or rather all the time. At least, in context of media and communication tools, we live in the age of plenty. From ads to AI, billboards to bots, and 360 degree to predictive advertising, communication is moving at a velocity and with a volume like never before.

Much of this is attributed to the digital, propelled by the global Internet penetration which is touted to be in the

3-billion-plus range, i.e., nearly 50 per cent of the world's population. We are seeing the worlds of Internet, big data and AI converging and the lines between e-commerce and ad platforms blurring.

The opportunities and challenges of this new media have changed the paradigm—for the marketers, creators and consumers. What makes it irresistible for marketers is real-time metrics and the nose-diving cost of acquisition per consumer, the crux being that whilst costs have plummeted, the reach has exploded. The rapid adoption of smart devices has accelerated the digital age. Monetization and usage are seeing an upward trajectory, given the innovative products and multiple touchpoints that are being spawned as we speak. Video and messaging have snowballed and new content types are being created; voice has provided another usage spike. Mobile advertising is also getting more and more share of the marketing and ad spend.

As advertisers, it is an exciting as well as complex time. From a creative perspective, digital and social media have redefined 'content'. With brands focusing on connecting directly with consumers across social platforms, the fuel they need to create and maintain their ability to connect, is content. Memes, clickbait, trending posts and hashtags testify to the growing demand of more creative assets, created economically and more frequently to bolster the continual presence of brands across platforms.

Initially, in the advertising industry, we saw a distinction, which some would contend was an artificial one: Creative assets designed for 'traditional' paid media distribution and 'content' for social or non-traditional distribution. There exists a concrete drive for consumer engagement through ideas that are 'social by design' and, therefore, considered different at inception. Yes, different platforms do have their distinct codes so to speak. However, insightful and relevant content is a great leveller.

There is definitely much discussion around AI and its impact on content. Technology is changing so rapidly that creativity and amusement can be confused. It's not tech but craft that has the power to say the same thing again and yet sound fresh. Creativity is not science, its art. AI and data is science, and science may go hand in hand with art, but let's not confuse the two.

> AI's inability to experience raw emotion, which humans have, will form the crux of the 'AI versus human creativity' debate.

AI, in advertising, may feed on a lot of material that has been done before, and would do permutations and combinations to create fresh things out of that material. But writers and creative people don't do permutations and combinations of work done before. With AI, I feel it would be difficult to touch upon an emotion which has never been touched upon before. Most importantly, when you are developing AI, you are feeding in an 'already been expressed' emotion. AI's inability to experience raw emotion, which humans have, will form the crux of the 'AI versus human creativity' debate in time.

However, apart from discussions around human and machine or medium-specific content, we need to step back and see what kind of a phenomenon is unfolding before our eyes, especially in the Indian context. On one hand, with 450 million Internet users, we are the second-largest online market; on the other, India has the fastest-growing newspaper industry amidst a global newspaper market that is stagnant. So, whilst digital media is growing exponentially, traditional media remains resilient. Is there a no man's land between traditional and digital media or are the borders porous? While the digital chorus is growing, another medley of TV, radio and outdoor plays simultaneously. In the US in 2017, the holy grail of TV advertising, the Super Bowl, saw marquee names like Doritos and Mountain Dew missing from the pack of advertisers. Switch to the Indian Premier League in India, where each nanosecond on TV is sold for unmentionable amounts and every brand worth their sales figures, is featured. Is it a 'developed versus developing' country phenomenon?

Well, it's not that simple. Fact is, India is at a cusp of a colossal transformation. The answer, as far as I am concerned, lies in the heart of India—rural and semi-urban India. In this context, a key aspect that we in India, particularly, cannot ignore is that of mobile content. It is growing at a phenomenal rate, literally adding thousands at the next glance. Though rural India, with a population of approximately 900 million, currently has only 200 million Internet users, the disparity is large. This shouldn't be seen as just a gap, but the quantum of potential and opportunity. For here, the Internet and mobile is not just another mode of contact or entertainment, but a tool to empower.

What we are witnessing is a democratization of communication and knowledge. The thrust, of course, is on infrastructure and bandwidth. But even if that does not develop at breakneck speed, opportunity for brands is still huge. We know that penetration of smartphones is still not that high but as costs drop, we will see the shift from feature to smart in no time. The economics will make this segment very lucrative for marketers, who will have to cater with finer and finer differential digital strategies for rural consumers, be it languages or a simpler app designed for smaller screens and bandwidths. As advertisers, we need to attune ourselves

> 'The medium is the message' approach only takes us so far; the crux will be in moulding the medium.

more finely to the next big wave of consumer understanding and content creation.

We are a complex country where contradictions coexist. Some decades ago, TV had eclipsed the print and radio style of communication, bringing forth a new audio-visual language. Similarly, it's time that we understand and look at rural-relevant content specifically as these new Internet/mobile consumers do not identify with the urban consumption patterns nor relate to dominant language codes. The focus will need to be on content that is relatable and relevant to rural India. Nearly half of India's mobile phone users own smartphones and their expectation to be served through this medium on their own terms will only escalate. This 'mobile-first' culture will have its impact on not just media, gaming and entertainment, but sectors, industries and segments that will transform lives in rural India—be it health, education or agriculture. Films (long form/short form), news, gaming, music, education, information, e-commerce—all have to understand and develop accordingly. Be it e-chaupals, banking, shopping, entertainment, vernacular content is key. Also, there will be a rapid move towards individualization of content as against the current trend of consuming content in groups. Each consumer's experience, like for their urban cousins, will be designed using intuitive data tools. We need to understand that this audience will be a combination of a small-town India with a rural cultural context, who have the aspirations and life goals of a First World country.

As advertisers, amidst these exciting times of change, what should be kept firmly in sight are not just percentages and the altering media and content scape, but how the brand story will cut across. Brands have to think deeply on how strong their product offering is and whether the brand has a life truth that is steeped in the consumer consciousness, for only then will it resonate. 'The medium is the message' approach only takes us so far; the crux will be in moulding the medium.

I am truly excited to see this new change unfolding. As a creative person, there is nothing like the next big frontier.

13

Artificial Intelligence and Advait

Several forms of AI and machine learning exist: From narrow AI, which can interpret video feeds from drones carrying out visual inspections of landmines, to general/strong AI, which is capable of applying intelligence to *any* problem, rather than a specific one. On the other hand, we have human intelligence or consciousness, which, to my mind, is about various stimuli and the reactions to those stimuli—essentially a unique response to unique situations. I'm not trying to define being 'human' here, but simply exploring, in the context of AI, what a 'human being' means.

From my vantage point, in the above context, a human being is all about a corpus of experiences, and a collection of responses and decisions. It's these which make a particular human being unique, giving him/her a certain characteristic. It's about understanding a simple correlation: That in a particular situation, this particular human being reacts in this particular way.

For AI, all of the above is seen as data. Everything related to a human—his/her memories, narratives, habits and reactions—are data for AI. And if this data is available sans the physical body, a human being can be recreated. For, if one part of the human being is body and the other is consciousness, the latter is replicable, because in the world of tech, this consciousness is nothing but a set of data. So, if this data is accessible, then so is the human being—in terms of his/her set of reactions and responses. In a nutshell, AI can pre-empt human behaviour and predict human reaction, as all kinds of data are collectively available. Though many an artist, and all those who believe in an X factor, may be doubtful about this simplification of human life and of AI's ability to recreate human consciousness, it cannot be completely written off.

So, can AI truly predict human behaviour? In my opinion, to a certain extent, yes. Soon, we will see a lot of constructive uses of AI in the real world, both in the

> *We have heard, that no matter how different or diverse we feel, deep down we are products of the same consciousness.*

everyday and in specific situations. For example, as an individual, when you are faced with a problem, your reaction to that problem, and the solution, comes from your available knowledge or the information stored in your mind. Say, a fire alarm goes off and immediately you understand that you have to vacate the building. This is what you have learnt, and this is the information that your internal system has brought to bear.

But what happens if your reactions and solutions are not limited to, or emerging from, your knowledge and experiences alone?

In the world of AI, the know-how of innumerable others is also available. So, AI's response and reaction are multifold, more informed and more aware. It has access to shared learnings, collective capabilities and skills. Therefore, it is not possible to compare a single human being's learnings to that of an aggregated base.

It is, no doubt, fascinating; more so when I see a link between this very advanced, cutting-edge tech reality and the eternal mysticism of India—the fundamentals of spirituality the way we have learnt it in this part of the world. 'Advait'—nondual, 'not two'—this oneness is a fundamental quality, which means that everything is a part of, and made up of, one nondual consciousness. *'Ek noor te sab jag upjeya'* (from one light, came the entire creation). Some of us have grown up with philosophies and phrases like 'a "human being" is a thought projection of the cosmic mind'. We have heard, that no matter how different or diverse we feel, deep down we are products of the same consciousness, and we are all connected through this energy and consciousness.

Here, let me take creative licence for a while: At times, you may experience an inexplicable urge to cry for no apparent reason—not induced by any specific problem or pain point, and simply feeling sad for no reason. Some may call this a chemical imbalance, and doctors could diagnose this as a secretion of a particular enzyme. But I want to look at it a little differently. Perhaps, this feeling is experienced because some human being, in some part of the world, is going through intense pain. You may not know about this person, nor be aware of his/her situation, but you feel the pain because the central—the collective—consciousness senses it; and thus, being a part of this shared consciousness, you are impacted.

> *The creative piece of work reflects the granular, since it was a first-hand experience.*

It seems the concept of having access to all that has been thought of, created or experienced, is possible if you are 'plugged in' to the larger source. Great masters of the world have often said that meditation is nothing but tuning yourself into the eternal consciousness. If you are attuned, then the benefits of an eternal energy reservoir can be found. I find a similarity between this thought process and AI, which also tunes you into the larger source.

We are in an ecosphere today, where we carry around, in our pocket, the information, knowledge and experiences of the world. This is already challenging our education systems, which were based on rote and text learning. Interpretation and application—rather than retention of information—is the focus now. The human mind is now more valued for this processing power, than storage.

At this point, let me change gears. In some fields, like research, diagnostics, navigation systems and so on, the application of this collective knowledge is a natural fit. However, I feel that there are some areas which are not easily definable and where AI may not have it all figured out—at least, not yet. Let's take the example of Benjamin, a 'bot' that is experimenting with writing screenplays. I understand that the bot's AI would have access to every script created and every situation encountered, from which it can possibly create endless permutations and combinations to arrive at a desired scene. Yes, you will see a scene in front of you, designed by collective intelligence. But where all of this doesn't sit too comfortably in neat boxes of configuration is the source of inspiration.

Think of a writer who had to go for a cremation of a near one. Willing himself to face the burning pyre, he registers people's faces visible through the filter of the flames. The smoke-induced tears intermingle with those that well up from feeling emotional. He hears the crackles of the wood which is ablaze, and is suddenly taken aback by the strong odour of burning flesh—a smell so intense, so primal, that it permeates the very being. Later, whilst picking up the pen or tapping the keyboard, the source of what he pours out, is an amalgamation of the mixed visuals and emotions that have been witnessed and felt. The creative piece of work reflects the granular, since it was a first-hand experience.

This first-hand experience is unavailable to AI. It is able to access expression, but not the tactile, sensorial experience.

> *AI is able to access expression, but not the tactile, sensorial experience.*

That is where the difference lies. There is no replacement of first-hand experience and the nuanced complexity with which we humans experience life—at least, yet. AI will have to struggle a bit here. But in many other areas, the possibilities of AI are boundless.

14

Art and Responsibility: Is Art Independent of Societal Constraints?

It's a privilege that we humans have the gift of expression. And when this expression emerges with a nuanced rhythm, form and meaning, it is art—and we can't help but stand in awe. Along with this gift of self-expression comes the desire to make this creation resonate with others. Herein lies the conundrum. For, at times, this expansion of expression also becomes the breeding ground for obfuscation and contention, one where art meanders into the vortex of controversy.

Thoughts, words, ideas and I share an old, intimate

relationship. Art and creativity is what I stand by and always will. Additionally, over the past few months, a newer perspective has begun to unfold—one that asked of me as a creative person to not just exercise my artistic licence and brush aside mundane materiality, but intricately understand the overt and the subliminal aspects of expression.

I believe that the freedom to create and express is linked to the very grain of human existence. To simply take this for granted, without delving deep or being open to nuance is injustice to the warp and weft of life, especially in a culture like ours where expression's overt oeuvre is manifest in every fragment of our lives.

Whether in the soaring heights of imagination or the depths of thought and philosophy, the new and varied have always been embraced in uncountable examples of unfettered thought. Today, this freedom for some seems to have gathered an aggressive tenor which belies more than artistic integrity. Societal requests to explore whether an expression willingly or unwillingly impacts the society negatively, meets with a more than vociferous contention of freedom of expression. And equally vociferously, the same freedom to express a reaction is

> *To organize ourselves as a society and become 'civilized' was a 'universal' agreement among races.*

claimed by a section of the society.

Why do we see art and societal structures looking at each other with scepticism? It is because there's a trust deficit. Artists, to begin with, do not create to harm anyone. They express what they feel. The receivers of this art, too, do not think there is any other agenda or vested interests at play, for, in an intrinsically connected society, there is little mistrust.

It's when the relationship gets strained, that suspicion creeps in. In these circumstances, thoughts don't remain just an exploration, and art, not mere expression. A chasm appears, for there is a cloud of confusion over the basics.

Perhaps, some exploration is due here. Societies were products of collective choice. To organize ourselves as a society and become 'civilized' was a 'universal' agreement among races. We arrived at a certain code of conduct which, though at times in conflict with our innate instinct, is still willy-nilly adhered to, because, if our natural instincts are given carte blanche, formal structures of civil society may have little or no room. The understanding is that individual freedom will exist within a co-created civilizational code.

Civilization is a construct, but by collective choice. Sure, the role of art is to push boundaries, break templates, introduce fresher thought, and, in this process, some feathers are bound to be ruffled. But, overall, the freedom of individual expression comes bundled with a quid pro quo—an obligation of concern and sensitivity for the whole.

So, then, is art for society, or society for art? The question to contend with is straightforward: Apart from self-expression, should art that is made ostensibly for society at large, be sensitive to the society or not? This question becomes more pertinent when we talk of a particular art form, say commercial art or cinema, which demands a lot from the recipient—time, attention and money. In this context, should raising an expectation or concern be deemed akin to smothering the freedom of individual expression?

When a genuine piece of art emerges from the very being of the artist, its tide is unabated by box office fate or balance-sheet boundaries—free of the arithmetic of commerce. However, content that is created with the overarching principle of profit maximization needs to be seen in its own context. It does not imply that commercial art is a lesser form; simply, that the raison d'être is different, and the two should be seen as distinct.

> *Freedom is not a blank cheque; it comes with a fair barter of responsibility.*

Artistic licence should not be up for sale. If this clarity is lost, then for financial greed and narrow interests, there will be a trade-off of the common good. As a consequence, fault lines appear and corrode the fabric of society. Some of our artistic brethren often refer to Western societies, choosing with subtle ingenuity, examples which juxtapose Indian society as lacking in comparison. It's put forth volubly that the West's openness in all spheres of life and art be emulated.

Perhaps, a vital aspect is being missed. A genuine artist knows, that like true art, an authentic society is unique in thought and form. It has its own collective consciousness, one in which aeons of human experiences have cast their impression. Without a pregnant past, you can't have an effervescent present. After all, the present is not a singular suspended moment; it's a shoot that bursts forth from the womb of a continuum. To plaster one society's consciousness onto a uniquely different one is not constructive.

Conversely, when our creative work, especially cinema, is not acclaimed either critically or commercially on the world stage, the refrain often is that it caters to the sensibilities of our country/society, and the stamp of Western approval is not required.

Is that a naked dichotomy or an inconvenient truth? Whichever way one looks at it, every society carries with itself its identity and dynamics. Elements that need to be weeded out and ones that need nurturing have to be in context—of the indigenous and the universal, the individual and the collective.

Unfortunately, every such person who urges others to pay heed to the collective viewpoint, apart from that of the individual, is deemed as an enemy of the freedom of expression. Why does it become wrong to think about those not as empowered and privileged; vulnerable children; respecting each other's faith and beliefs; and being compassionate? Freedom is not a blank cheque; it comes with a fair barter of responsibility. Eventually, life trumps art and every true artist recognizes that and is sensitive to not just oneself but to the faintest murmurs in society. He or she knows that they are not more important than humanity. Inks would dry and brushes would stiffen in the face of one genuine tear drop or a mute cry of pain.

> *To assert one's own voice as civilized and decry every other as uncivilized, is condescension.*

There seems to be a broad understanding of the consumption format of the creative world. But then, the granularity and uniqueness of various consumption formats need to be understood better. For example, there is a huge difference between the manner in which content is consumed on the Internet and a film collectively viewed in a theatre. A person's personal viewing and a crowd's collective viewing are two different scenarios with distinct ramifications. The Internet is essentially for private viewing. Cinema, in a theatre, is viewed publicly. A crowd's collective mentality and reactions differ from that of an individual's, and needs to be paid heed to.

The Internet of Things is a space where both the beneficial and the detrimental exist. Shouldn't the latter be more finely evaluated—especially when it comes to children—for content that may not be age appropriate? Sure, all is available *on* the Internet but should our all be available *for* the Internet? We should not lose sight of the way ahead—not even in the din made by those who are called 'fringe groups'.

Let's deliberate on why these voices of 'fringe groups' are emerging. Fingers are often pointed at the politics of power. There is merit in the contention, but this is not the sole reason. There is more to think about here. And I say this, despite the fact that one has been at the receiving end (for giving the green signal for the release of the film *Padmaavat*).

Infuriated and saddened as I was at the violent protest against this movie, it's dishonest to not to see the complete picture. The entire world is going through a period of change; the manner in which we are linked to technology today is unprecedented. There are multiple platforms available for different voices. Those who see this as a problem are essentially the ones who believed that these platforms were exclusive, and so, kept these tools and platforms under control, mastering the codes and lexicon, and forgetting that there are others in the society, whose point of view may be a different one. Denying the existence of an alternate point of view, the moniker of fringe or lumpen elements is often applied to contrarian voices.

Let me be categorical here: The context here is of voicing one's concerns, not that of resorting to violence in any form. But to consider oneself as extraordinary just because one practises an art form and others as deficient in both sense and sensibility, and to assert one's own voice as civilized and decry every other as uncivilized, is condescension.

> Art, society, systems and freedom are all contextual, all work in progress, like ourselves.

The truth is that a society that is concerned for the larger good, has a connect with each stakeholder; there is mutual faith and the fundamental belief that our joys and sorrows are linked, as are our lives. This trust between an artist and society should never derail.

My intention is to share a perspective and evoke thought, and through a process of introspection and internal churn, understand the change around us in terms of both the personal and the collective. Let there be constant shaping, reshaping, augmenting and pruning. After all, art, society, systems and freedom are all contextual, all work in progress,

SECTION 3

Void and Celluloid

C*inema, over the last century, has welded itself into the cultural narrative. It achieved what no other medium could do before: It arrested the eyes, ears and mind, and transported us to newer worlds and the new worlds to us. Cinema changed the ways in which stories were told and consumed, forever. Indian films and their songs have subliminally defined the societal landscape, at times reflecting it and at others, shaping it—often for the better but sometimes for the worse. Their impact and their fault lines are fascinating.*

15

Fundamentals of Entertainment Products

A friend of mine from the film fraternity questioned the protest against films at a recent forum. Irate about why the entertainment industry is targeted to make a point, he wondered why other kinds of trade relations with hostile countries are not dealt with the same intensity.

As marketers, brand custodians and communication specialists, we need to decode this popular sentiment more intricately than merely painting it with a broad brushstroke of nationalism or anti-nationalism.

UNDERSTANDING ENTERTAINMENT PRODUCTS

Is there something different about the entertainment industry? The answer is a resounding 'yes'. We cannot equate the entertainment industry with other industries. Here, the products are unique: A result of various layers drawn from society. Its ingredients are not easily quantifiable; for, they are borrowed from existence—the ever-evolving, ever-changing river of life. Each piece of entertainment you create is 'mukhtalif', or different from the one you created previously.

On the other hand, standardization is the need in many other product categories. You don't need toothpaste to surprise you in the morning; you don't need a favourite comfort meal to astonish you every time you consume it.

But when it comes to entertainment products, 'surprise' needs to be an element. The product needs to challenge, motivate, thrill and, perhaps, even make one introspect. The expectations here are extremely high.

TV: A STAPLE; CINEMA: A STIMULANT

Sure there is a need for the less exciting and surprising variety as well—'comfort-ainment'. Indian TV has occupied this niche in the life of the consumer. It provides them staple entertainment, which is less unpredictable, less experimental in nature, has familiarity of characters and emotions, and a reaffirmation of belief. Such programming lulls, inducing a passive state. Very rarely you will find this genre of entertainment trying to challenge your thinking. It will constantly keep striking a known chord. But this genre aside, people's expectations from larger-scale entertainment products are quite varied. The spectrum ranges from a spectacle, to shades of drama, fantasy and mystique thrown in.

It's a far cry from the generation of audience which was mesmerized with even a DD *Krishi Darshan*, or took to learning Hindi to just be able to read Devkinandan Khatri's *Chandrakanta*, or waited with bated breath for a Friday movie release for their entertainment fix. There existed an entertainment deficit and the marginal utility was very high. Today's satiated generation has an entertainment surplus, which then makes it even more challenging than ever before to amuse and stimulate.

> *Today's satiated generation has an entertainment surplus, which then makes it even more challenging... to amuse and stimulate.*

Evolving expectations aside, let's delve a bit more into why entertainment products cannot simply be equated with other categories and why they become marked more readily for polemic politics.

SYMBOLS

Let's look at this through the lens of symbols. Certain kinds of symbols—political, national, religious, revolutionary—are a congregation of emotions in one place. By altering or embracing them, the intent is easily communicated. An ideology gets identified with a few codes. In the world of communication and brand-building, companies spend millions to establish their identity through symbols, be it their logo, colour or sound mnemonic.

People often utilize symbols as communication tools. The chances of popular entertainment being used as a tool to express a certain sentiment—in this case, nationalistic, and in others, anti-nationalistic—are very high.

THE UNIQUENESS OF THIS SYMBOL

I will refrain from a discussion on the genesis of this feeling, as there could be various sources of this sentiment: From an underlying sense of being wronged, to the socio-political atmosphere the world over. However, clearly, entertainment products occupy a distinct space in the imagination of the people, a space larger than what any other consumer brand can ever occupy. Most consumer brands desire to have a similar impact on the minds and hearts of the people. Brand custodians want their taglines, phrases and jingles to have the same recall power as entertainment products do. A popular film star gets hired, a trendy film musician is roped in, and a contemporary film director is brought in to recreate the magic they've created within the cinema industry.

But often, it doesn't work. Of course, there have been a few cases when there has been a fantastic popular connect with the consumer brand's communication, but they are rare. What is often forgotten is that popular culture is unique, is intrinsically linked to life and reflects its contextuality. The themes and content picked up are edgier, deeper, riskier—for example, films like *Garam Hawa*, *Bandini*, *Arth*, *Aandhi*, *Parzania*, *Bandit Queen*, *Satya*, *Rang De Basanti* and *Aarakshan*. Other consumer products steer clear of making social and political statements and remain neutral. They often navigate the safer, 'fuzzier' world. But cinema and popular culture thrive on live issues. They make use of the socio-political environment and have a big impact on minds and markets.

> As far as entertainment products are concerned, in an industry with a balance sheet, art is more commercial.

COMMERCIAL ART

Let's fine-tune our discussions regarding popular culture and cinema as symbols, and of art being marketed. When art is packaged and sold as a commercial product, it is not pure art any longer.

As far as entertainment products are concerned, in an industry with a balance sheet, art is more commercial. We are not talking about self-expression alone here; we are talking of a carefully crafted product for the consumer.

It would have been a very different scenario had we been discussing Muktibodh or Van Gogh. Where self-expression is the dominant emotion and not profitability or commercial success; where an intense inner compulsion exists and creation takes place regardless of consequence; where market forces matter little; where a restless soul is in the quest of finding meaning, not money, out of life—the canvas in these cases is larger than the balance sheet. And it's important for humanity that this unadulterated introspection and expression take place unhindered.

One cannot, and is not, undermining the calibre of popular-genre products here. For, even in commercial art, there have been and are, instances of staggering self-expression and some of them are deliciously poised between art and commerce. But there is surely a difference when you tailor-make an entertainment product after analysing what people want, and try to press convenient buttons aimed to please or cater to the lowest common denominator. It would be myopic to believe that people do not see this variance.

In a free world, traffic flows both ways. As much as we have the freedom to express and create what we wish to share or market, the other forces, too, will exercise their freedom to leverage it.

As we proceed into a fractured future, different points of view will collide and different streams of thinking will come face to face.

16

Bollywood: A Spectacle Beyond Entertainment?

Movies rest on the boundary between dreams and reality. Their very nature of engagement—that of casual distraction—carries, ironically, the tools to disarm. Movies bypass our preset frame of mind and defence mechanisms; we engage with them with no guardedness or scrutiny. They can take us on a flight of fantasy or that of self-discovery; they can suspend logic or echo emotions. The magic of cinema has touched us all. But have films transcended to a function beyond? Are we, as a society, looking for movies as medicine?

First, let us understand the nature of Bollywood movies.

Barring a few films that have raised serious questions and issues, Bollywood has always been a spectacle, a grand 'tamasha'. And the staple of Bollywood has been entertainment—so, you have your favourite hero and heroine, songs and dances, predictable situations.

I am often asked, especially in the West: Why does Bollywood keep repeating the same storyline in most of its films? My answer is: In Hindi films, it's not about 'what', but 'how'. In the first fifteen minutes of the film, you know who's going to get the girl and who's going to be killed. Nobody needs to be told that the hero will overcome all obstacles or that the villain is going to die at the end of the film.

Is Bollywood capable or desirous of driving social change, or is it a mere reflection of society?

The question is: How? That's the key. And the 'how' is played out through the dialogue, lyrics and songs. That's where the entertainment comes in.

'*Tere paas aake mera waqt guzar jaata hai.*
Do ghadi ke liye gham jaane kidhar jaata hai.'

The above lyrics of a song from the movie *Neela Aakash* (1965) aptly captures this sentiment—it's a momentary release. Of course, you can argue that this is escapism, but then, what isn't? When one plays with their child, they forget that they have a boss, troublesome clients or loan instalments to be paid. That is a kind of escapism, too.

So, while classically, Bollywood films don't set out to be therapeutic, they offer release in a different sense. It is at one end, an easy suspension of our reality, giving us a 'little vacation' from the mundane and, perhaps, a fresh perspective. But it is fleeting.

Once in a while, however, comes along a film that is more than that. You leave the movie hall but not the film. You carry its emotions, its imagery and its imprint. It makes you reflect, perhaps on your own life experiences, or raises serious questions—for example, movies like *Mother India*, *Mazdoor*, *Pyaasa* or, in recent times, *Rang De Basanti*. These are films that have connected to the audience at various levels, and have provoked debate and introspection.

Thus, the intriguing issue arises again: Is cinema, especially Indian cinema, capable of driving societal change or sparking a behavioural trend; or is it a mere reflection of the society? While the former may be deemed by some as optimism or even hubris, to weigh in for the latter is perhaps too simplistic. Having said that, what is clear is that the manner in which a cinematic offering is consumed is dependent on the phase that the social order is going through.

Today's society is looking for constant gratification. Like a child who becomes bored of a new toy in a few hours and is immediately on the lookout for another, the media and people are quick to pick up an issue, lap it up, extract all the juice out of it and discard it when the next topic comes along.

Society is looking for that quick adrenaline rush and wants to consume it without actually going through the experience. Consumers want virtual gratification and movies provide them that. It is role-playing of a kind. You could watch a film about, say, corruption, and it will make your blood boil, but you don't have to go out and do anything about it. Or, infidelity may not be relevant to your life but when you see a movie that talks about it, you experience it vicariously. And at the end of the film, you can come out of the theatre, have a conversation about it and experience a certain satisfaction.

> *The manner in which a cinematic offering is consumed is dependent on the phase that the social order is going through.*

Films, by their very nature, package situations in narratives which can become the basis for discussion before, during and after their viewings. That's why the 'how' of Bollywood is important. For instance, if a C-grade film tackles the subject of infidelity or promiscuity (which they do quite often), it is not taken as a social statement. This is because that is not the intention; titillation is. But if a film like *Arth*, *Silsila* or *Let's Talk* deals with these subjects, it does so with the intention of making a point and that sets you thinking.

One must understand the difference between virtual gratification and a genuine connect. In the case of *Rang De Basanti*, there was a real connect with the youth. It stirred them and provoked them to think. As one of the characters says, it made him feel that he was not dead yet: '*Main mara nahin abhi tak*'. It talked about the enemy within the country and self; about throwing out the enemies of today just as colonial power had been, decades ago. Watching that film was like being part of a mass protest—one had the satisfaction of having taken a stand. An effective film makes you introspect, forces you to think and ask yourself questions, and ignites a passionate debate. That's what *Rang De Basanti* did.

The quality of films being made does echo, in part, the state that culture finds itself in at the time. When mainstream movies, which are allegedly catering to urban sensibilities, sell well-packaged tripe, our culture suffers. When mediocrity is greeted gushingly by the box office, the more evolved prospects putrefy. When our writers and artists seem unable to honestly deal with emotional subject matter, our cinematic language languishes.

While, for some, films mirror their own reality and resonate with their own life and feelings, for the larger section, they provide a momentary high, a quasi-satisfaction. But films do not set out to be therapeutic. At the end of the day, they are just entertainment and only some amongst them are more than that. The only qualm is that the latter are too few and far between.

17

The Melodies of Life

The scene is vivid in my memory: Early one morning, on a worn out but comfortable chair in a B&B cottage, Assisi city, Italy, I sat with a cup of coffee warming my hands. Suddenly, I hear that unmistakable birdsong, 'ku-ku-ku...kuku'. A pervasive warmth envelops and instantly transports me miles and decades into the past.

When I was a young boy, of eight or nine, wandering in the woods, collecting pine fruit in Almora, the same melody rang in my ears... 'ku-ku-ku...kuku', mixed with the gentle voice of my nani, recounting the story related to this birdsong.

The story goes thus:

A young Pahadi woman was married into a family in a far-off village. She eagerly awaits a yearly visit by her beloved brother on the occasion of Bhai Dooj (a festival to celebrate the bond between brothers and sisters). Starting from his home in the village, at the crack of dawn, the brother leaves on an empty stomach, as per custom, to eat or drink only after his sister has adorned his forehead with a teeka (a turmeric mark). Walking arduously along the mountain tracks for hours, he arrives at his sister's house.

Meanwhile, exhausted with the day's chores, the young sister involuntarily slips into a slumber while waiting for him.

On arriving, the brother looks affectionately at his sleeping sister, tenderly draws a blanket up to her chin, caresses her forehead and, not wanting to spoil the precious period of her much deserved rest, leaves.

> *(Songs) signify the faith that, amongst the many challenges, life is still beautiful—there is much to live for.*

After a while, the sister awakens and on finding that her brother had come and left, weeps inconsolably, saying, 'My brother came, tired and hungry, and left... and all I did was sleep.' Wallowing in guilt, she dies, yearning for her brother. It is she who is reincarnated as the Ghughuti bird and coos her plight: '*Ghughuti basuti, baeh bhuk go main sooti*' (my brother left, hungry, and I kept sleeping).

This story of the 'ghughuti basuti'—the bird and its song—has become a part of folklore. I grew up regarding this bird and the song as something unique to my part of the world. I was somewhat jolted but very intrigued on hearing the familiar sound in a small town in Italy. Maybe there was another narrative related to this bird's song in this country. But even if there wasn't, it did not take away the beauty and pathos of the story. The tale of the 'ghughuti basuti' may have been born out of someone's imagination but it had become a strong tie for me… a link to my childhood and memories associated with it.

Such is the power of stories and songs. They feed your soul and forge beautiful bonds. In the everyday world of challenges, banalities and prosaic conversations, the human mind and heart craves for gentler emotion and it expresses this through a touching story, beautiful poetry or a lilting song. These fulfill our need for a softer world. Songs can be therapeutic, inspiring, philosophical, or just a gentle bond. To me, they signify the faith that, amongst the many challenges, life is still beautiful—there is much to live for.

This is the reason I like writing songs. They rekindle belief in life. It is simply fascinating to know how deep the connection between song and society is. There is no cultural group—no matter how remote or isolated—that does not sing. Not only are songs ancient and universal, they are linked to vital matters—to invoke and eulogize gods, to celebrate rites of passage and recount historic sagas or just as a means of personal expression. Songs find an inimitable niche in our lives.

Songs have functioned as 'carriers of culture' in Indian traditions. Our scriptures and epics are mostly in verse; the couplets of Kabir and Rahim, and the songs of Mira and Lal Ded, are a part of our oral tradition; age-old wisdom is passed on through generations, via rhymes and songs; and our performing arts—including folk theatre in the form of nautankis, 'jatras' (Bengali folk theatre) and many similar forms—are replete with songs.

Moving on, what perhaps concerns us more, are the times and aspects we can relate to. In our time, the influence and universal connect of cinema is difficult to miss. It is a significant phenomenon that has developed into a potent and versatile art form. Multiple creative expressions, be that of drama, poetry, design and a host of other arts, find a platform in cinema.

Music—a source of religious inspiration, cultural expression as well as entertainment—is an integral part of Indian cinema. In fact, there have been very few Hindi films without any songs. Today, in the environment of experimental cinema, 'crossover' themes and globalization, it is the music and songs of our films that are acknowledged as a defining characteristic of our cinema.

I have often pondered over this unique bond between songs and Indian cinema. Perhaps, this intrigues me even more because I came to this field without any roots or background in the world of films. I am an outsider who chanced upon this industry.

My childhood and much of adulthood were spent in Almora, in the lap of nature and the majestic Himalayas. Films and their music found little place in our home, where the atmosphere was that of Hindustani classical music and endearing folk music. Life in the mountains was a source of inspiration, and writing stories, poetry and prose came naturally to me as a child. I have a very fond memory of those days: I wrote stories during our summer holidays and compiled them in small handbound books that became a part of the self-created 'Prasoon Bal Pustakalaya'—a circulating library. A princely sum of ₹1 charged for each booklet I wrote, went on to make my childhood richer in myriad ways.

But as I grew up—the vibrant creative atmosphere of home notwithstanding—parental wisdom made it clear that writing and music were not viable career options. My father was clear that poetry would not provide the means in the real world. That's the time when, despite little interest, I took the decision to pursue the conventional path of formal education—a science degree and then an MBA. Looking back, I often wonder why I didn't go against my parents' wishes and pursue my passion. It is perhaps simpler to focus on individual goals and aspirations but that seemed selfish and thoughtless to me then. I just couldn't be insensitive enough to rebel.

However, I did not find business management stimulating enough and was unsure about the path that lay ahead. Being placed in a typical 9-to-5 job environment was anathema to me, and I literally ran away from an interview call from a paint company. Then, one fine day, a very unique company arrived at our institute to recruit summer trainees. I learnt that there exists a field of work called communication and advertising—a profession in which I could employ a combination of my training in business management and my interests in literature, writing, poetry and music. Until then, I didn't know what I could do with my passions. Most of the art forms that I loved had relevance in advertising. This was where I would get paid to write—a dream come true! However, I was still uncertain and confused about the path I had chosen because mass media communication as a career option was comparatively new, not very well established and found few takers. Films and music albums were still nowhere in the range of my radar of thought.

> *The content of our songs, in many a case, can effortlessly find itself in the same realm as poetry and literature.*

When I look back on this phase, I feel it is important to be confused in life—it is a significant stage. The trauma and frustration one experiences during that time is a personal journey, one where you understand your strengths and strike a balance between what you want to do and what ought to be done. The lack of a fixated mindset and the initial lack of clarity made me explore, experiment and tread an unconventional path. However, all through, my love for writing remained an integral part of my existence.

There was no plan or desire to write for films. I loved music and would spend all my free time in and around Kamani Auditorium in Delhi, listening to classical music concerts till the wee hours. I stayed in the outskirts of Delhi and the bus service ceased after eleven at night and one had to wait till five or six in the morning for the service to resume. So, after many late-night concerts—drawing my jacket closer in the Delhi chill—I would huddle up and sleep contentedly on the bench at the bus stop, with the ragas reverberating in my head!

It was during this phase that I met some like-minded people and dabbled in writing songs for bands like Silk Route and musicians like Shubha Mudgal. Writing for music albums was more to do with giving voice to the poet in me and did not have any commercial underpinnings.

My work in the music albums was noticed by a film director—Rajkumar Santoshi—and he approached me to write a song. However, I was more excited about the fact that the famed musician Ilaiyaraaja would be composing and Lataji would be singing my song, rather than the fact that I had got an opportunity to write for a Hindi feature film.

Writing lyrics hasn't been, and is not, my profession; it's a passion. It has enabled me to connect with sensitive connoisseurs of poetry and songwriting. Thus, my thoughts, approach and point of view about songwriting stem neither from a lineage, nor from a film background; they come purely from what I have perceived and experienced as a person and as a writer.

The endeavour here is to share some of my observations and understanding, simply as food for thought and perhaps as a glimpse into my world of music and song.

In my view, the Indian film industry has been prolific in diverse aspects—technical, production, direction, performances, and so on. But if we talk about music, it has been exceptional, and with respect to lyrics—par excellence. The content of our songs, in many a case, can effortlessly find a place in the same realm as poetry and literature. I say this as it is rare for a country to have literary writers and poets of legendary stature write for their feature films. It is fortunate that poets like Sahir Ludhianvi, Kaifi Azmi, Gopaldas 'Neeraj', Majrooh Sultanpuri, Pandit Narendra Sharma and Shailendra have enriched Indian cinema with their art. They understood the relevance of songs in our society. We belong to a culture which reads less but listens more. This oral tradition enriched our songs with philosophy, emotion, belief, ideals and deep symbolism.

The songs of every era are reflective of the morality of the times, the emotional temperature of that period and the intellectual and artistic talent they spawn and nurture. For example, the early 1930s and '40s seemed to have borrowed more from folk traditions, with dozens of songs weaving the narrative. Songs from the '50s reflected the optimism and idealism of nation-building; a slight societal disillusionment crept in in the '60s; and an overt expression and exuberance of a different generation clearly marked the '70s. But the cinema and songs that I recollect more vividly belong to the '80s and '90s—apart from some in the recent times. Apart from some exceptions, most of them seemed like a formula, much like 'stock' music. It was, in fact, the parallel music industry, in the form of popular music bands and solo artists, which I watched with much fascination. This gave me impetus and hope that unique talent can have a platform to create and express, independent of the constraints of the plot of a film. I wrote some of my most cherished songs for independent albums—*Ab Ke Saawan, Mann Ke Manjeere, Boondein*, etc. Unfortunately, the trend of an independent-from-films music platform could not sustain itself for long, commercially. This is one scenario that I would love to see change.

I say this because the room for individual expression in music needs to be explored more. While reality shows and other platforms offer a transient opportunity, the final destination for all artists remains cinema. The current times are witness to vibrant and diverse developments, be it in the field of politics, protests, social media, technological changes or the increasingly economically empowered and expressive youth. This trend should reflect even in the field of independent music, which has the potential to be the reflection and expression of our times.

It is also interesting to recall that while a parallel music industry was coming up in the '90s, there was also the advent of a distinct kind of voice—in popular songs like 'Achcha Sila Diya Tune Mere Pyaar Ka' or 'Tum To Thehere Pardesi'—which came from a very different social stratum. This trend has gained in strength in the present times. Nowadays, I often hear people lamenting about the quality of songs, citing that a baser language and voice are reflected in the many so-called item numbers. I don't think we can cast this phenomenon aside with disdain or merely embrace it as an index of our times. It needs to be analysed and understood.

> *I've struggled a lot to figure out what kind of work will satisfy the artist in me and yet find mass acceptance.*

It will be naïve on our part to think that these kind of songs did not exist in our society earlier. They did, but were perhaps confined to a limited audience. The social, economic and cultural hierarchy created an invisible wall. This compartmentalization—by design or default—did not easily allow a particular kind of music, voice and lyric to reach the middle-class drawing rooms and its sensibilities. Today, the mass market is expanding, walls between classes are coming down, and the wallet is democratizing taste. So, whether for the good or bad, all kinds of music are finding a place in the 'mainstream'.

Does this imply that we will see the very qualities that have defined our songs for generations being lost? Will there be an erosion of the lilting and hummable melodies, depth in lyrics and well-trained voices?

As I see it, the current times are both challenging and exciting for the industry. Whilst musicians, lyricists and artists need to accept the changing market demands and cater to many diverse tastes in the context of film songs, I believe we must strive to retain their core purity and quality. Songs have to move beyond the here and now of pure entertainment, for they have the potential to impact and shape popular consciousness and infuse it with sensitivity and thought.

For songwriters specifically, this balance for quality calls for more experimentation. I remember, when I first started writing for films, it was often commented that my use of words was very unusual. The staple words of Hindi film songs like 'dil', 'maahiya' and the like, were missing from my songs; instead, a different approach with songs like 'Masti Ki Paathshala' (*Rang De Basanti*) or 'Kaun Si Dor' (*Aarakshan*)—with rarely-used words like 'shashwat'—found expression. I guess it is a reflection of the fact that film music was not a part of my growing-up years. My vocabulary was a distillation of literature, folk music and the colloquial language I grew up with.

Many a time, I was and still am, told by producers and music directors that a particular word or phrase or composition 'will not work' or will not be easily understood. This is where I've struggled a lot to figure out what kind of work will satisfy the artist in me and yet find mass acceptance. During such times, I often wonder: Is love for music an acquired trait? If it is not, then how is it that what sounds like a beautiful piece of music to one person can become a cacophony to another? It is a fact that often some pieces of music—be it pure classical or folk—are not enjoyed in their pure form and have to be made palatable for a larger audience. Music from strings and saxophones, and certain chords have to be added to make it familiar and acceptable. Words are oversimplified—and in some cases, dumbed down with emphasis. Are we then dealing with conditioned minds that are culturally trained in one way or another? Is music, then, more of a reflex action—a habit?

At times, human reaction to music seems almost premeditated. It is, as if, a certain part of our brain deals with music and supplies a certain set of emotions and feelings. The majority buys a block of emotions instead of merely buying music. 'Nostalgia', 'romantic', 'spurned in love', 'devotional', 'techno', 'party', 'dance'—these are all categories of songs. A song is enjoyed not so much for its individual standing but as part of the bigger package of music. Cast in a familiar mould, a song evokes preconceived emotions that numb us into enjoying them.

The creative construction of a song—the complexity of composition, depth of lyrics or the intricacies of instrumentation—are rarely paid any attention to. The all-encompassing quality of 'entertainment' seems to have become the criteria for judging music and songs. This is perhaps a reflection of our times where shallow, instant gratification is given more prominence than the weight of content.

However, if this trend continues and the staple and 'instantly understandable' songs are demanded and settled for most of the times, the space for experimentation will continue to diminish. Perhaps this is the reason why a song like 'Kala Bandar' with phrases like *'Kasmein to moongphali hain, jab jee chahe hum khate'* (Promises are peanuts, we eat them on a whim)—though very potent and satirical in content—did not find as many takers as I thought it would.

A hip-hop manner of social commentary and satire is not what the Indian mass market is predisposed to.

But this must change and evolve. It is a fact that songs are a part of the narrative for a particular reason. The fun, 'frothy' song exists because of the need for a suspension of logic—a respite—and a philosophical song, for a kind of collective catharsis.

However, the room to explore a new dimension within the parameters of a given situation is something that the writer in me craves for. A 'given situation' is a phrase which brings a particular aspect to mind that I would like to dwell upon a bit here—the significance of love songs in our films. Romance has been the backbone of Indian film music and song, so much so that I've often wondered if love and romance have been a more significant aspect of our culture than any other, for they find expression in every second film song. Indian society is very layered; its social and moral fabric very intricate. The man-woman relationship is played out in the arena of social restriction and sanction.

Romance was traditionally a taboo and it found expression through poetry and song. However, the

> *Writing lyrics for films is like walking a tightrope... Striking the right balance is critical.*

boundaries of romance are expanding and they ought to. In fact, sooner or later, its expression will need to encompass same-gender romance, which, as of now, is limited to grudging acceptance and finds expression via comic amusement and irreverence. This trend should change; writing for same-gender romance has to be explored in a sensitive manner.

Another dynamic that is playing out in the songs of our times is that of a change in the use of language. As pointed out earlier, I have often been asked about the lack of regular words like 'jigar', 'jaanejaan', etc., in my lyrics. I don't try anything consciously. The fact is that one uses the language that comes most naturally to him or her. Some generations ago, it was a prevalent thought that romantic songs are best written in Urdu. But lyricists Bharat Vyas and Shailendra used Hindi beautifully to dispel this notion. Neeraj wrote the lilting 'Phoolon Ke Rang Se' with words like 'paati'.

Nowadays, the use of Hinglish is prevalent in Hindi film songs. English phrases have seeped into our songs and I am often asked to include them to make the song hip and contemporary. However, what must be understood is that the random use of English does not imply modernity. The thought has to be contemporary. The use of an archaic word like 'paathshala', in the song 'Masti Ki Paathshala', made it a much-loved song amongst the youth because it interestingly juxtaposed the legacy of indigenous language with their way of life, which is increasingly becoming modern and Westernized.

I feel, that for a language to flourish, it has to incorporate newer influences. There must be dynamism in it. It has to have 'gati'—a tide, a movement—like an ever-flowing stream. After all, *'Bhasha add gayi to sadd gayi'* (Language, if stagnant, turns stale).

Today, English words are used in everyday parlance, across various strata of society. Art needs to, and will, reflect changes in society. Of course, much is dependent on how the inclusion of English words is done. If it is just for effect, then it is bound to sound nonsensical, but if done interestingly and intelligently, it will find a unique connect.

Moving on, I am often asked what makes for a beautiful song. What came first: The tune or the words? For me, a soulful song is one that makes it impossible to decipher this; where there is no overt competition between the music and the lyrics; one that is just a beautiful blend. And I work towards creating this seamless quality. Also, I try not to succumb to the lure of the overt. Writing, or any other art form which makes the message explicit, is inherently lazy. Creativity and craft come in when the effect—and not the effort—behind it is apparent.

Portraying a specific situation and narrowing it down to achieve the exact connotation is the task often entrusted to songwriters. But to use it as a tipping point—a trigger—to be able to transcend the here and now of the situation, and to achieve a deeper, larger meaning, is the work of a master. As a situation, a scene depicting women languishing in a jail could have been apt for lyrics like *'Salaakhon ke peeche...kahin tod rahi hai ummeed dum'*; but lyrics like *'Ab ke baras bhej bhaiyya ko babul'* created an atmosphere so poignant that it not only evoked a lump-in-the-throat sentiment but found an identity beyond the film.

Another point of value to me is the unique ability—intentional or inherent—to let the viewer and listener own the song. After all, *'kaun rota hai kisi ke dukh mein? Har kisi ko apna gham yaad aaya'* (who cries for the other? All of us are reminded of our own pain seeing the other suffer). There has to be space for the listener to occupy and belong to that song. There has to be room for discovery, for the individual to get involved and derive his or her own interpretation from it.

Writing lyrics for films is like walking a tightrope—one cannot be vague and excessively symbolic like in poetry, but at the same time, the mystique and beauty should not be compromised. Striking the right balance is critical.

Thus, as a lyric writer, one needs to be careful about the metre, complex rhyme schemes and poetic images; yet the language has to be clear. One should have the ability to create a sense of wonder about the everyday. More importantly, this needs to be done without any pretension and without making the poetry needlessly inaccessible and difficult to understand.

This brings me back to the aspect of being a true music lover. The responsibility of a listener, too, comes into play here. The work we choose to celebrate, remember and nurture is a reflection of where we stand as people and as a society. A quest for familiarity and a fixed 'type' of music is against the very DNA of creative things. Genuine music lovers appreciate intricacy and hold in respect, work that embraces songwriting as an art form and not just three minutes of foot-stomping entertainment. The onus of quality work is as much on the listeners as on the creators.

A beautiful song is like a waft of air carrying the scent of the season. Even when the breeze has drifted afar, the fragrance remains. A creative person hands over a fragile creation to a listener, who, in turn, should be sensitive to a delicate melody, a heartfelt piece of writing. Only then can we create and accept classic and timeless songs—those that will find place in the glorious realm of Indian cinema—but most importantly, touch and remain a part of the lives of their listeners. Having said all this, I must confess that all of the above finds little space in my consciousness when I write. When I write, I just write. The blank white sheet of paper calls me, and holding my pen, I just let myself be led into a world of thoughts and feelings.

18

A Peek into the Hundred Years of Indian Cinema

Cinema all over the world has influenced viewers to a considerable degree, but the myriad ways in which Indian cinema—regional or Hindi—has had an impact through generations is unique. It has influenced popular consciousness in more ways than one—in the profound and the banal; in art and business; in the subtle shaping of thought and the outward expression of behaviour. The glorious journey of Indian cinema, now of over a hundred years—from the time of the first feature film to the recent ₹200-plus-crore-club phenomenon—brings flashes of plenteous thought and reflection to my mind.

CINEMA AND ITS AUDIENCES

The journey of Indian cinema has not been an easy one. It had to contend with many a challenge along the way. In the initial decades, there was a certain uniformity of approach. Cinema catered to, largely, middle-class sentiment and morality. There was also a wealth of literature that it drew from. The incredible raw material in the form of culturally relevant writing—like the works of Premchand and many luminaries from Bengal—was also a potent source of inspiration. In the years to come, those who wrote exclusively for the screen would find it difficult to match up to the depth and magnitude seen in literature. Also, in the initial phase, moving picture was a novelty and the limited middle-class audience was receptive to quality literary work and did not hanker for dumbed-down entertainment.

> *Cinema catered largely to the middle class and its morality, so the baser themes remained on the fringes.*

As times leapfrogged, there were newer segments that became the target audience—ones that had not necessarily been brought up on a diet of literature, poetry, music and fine art. Cinema had to face the challenge of widening the base and keeping its artistic sensibilities thriving. On one hand, it had to be a medium of the masses, and on the other, it had to be the channel that kept art alive. Cinema has struggled to strike a balance between these criteria.

Today, many lament the decline in the overall quality, citing examples of sensational storylines and the increased crassness of lyrics and song. I agree that the baser approach and triteness, and lack of thought and craft is extremely disturbing. But it would be naïve to think that this is a new phenomenon. This lewd nature of narratives and songs has always existed in a part of our society, but didn't find a way into the mainstream consciousness and sensibility. Cinema catered largely to the middle class and its morality, so the baser themes remained on the sidelines.

Contrary to the premise of a larger section of social strata now forming a part of the cinema-watching audience, it's interesting to note that representation of the non-urban audience is dimming. The portrayal of the 'aam aadmi' in cinema—barring a handful of films—is fading, and rural representation and voice from the villages in mainstream films is less visible and audible. From a wider perspective, this lacuna has given a new lease of life to the regional film industry. Take, for example, Marathi cinema, which is witnessing a mini renaissance, bringing forth some fresh sensibilities and subjects. Niche cinema is very good for art. It keeps alive the symbolic and nuanced form of cinema that becomes vulnerable in the battle for the larger share of the mighty commercial pie.

SILVER LINING

Even though there is a widening of the audience base and an arguable erosion in the depth of content, there is a silver lining. But this perspective would need to be tempered with my theory of the Cultural eye and the Organism eye. As discussed earlier, when one is initially faced with an object or instance, it's first consumed from their Cultural eye. We are unable to see the object as it really is and react to it based on an earlier frame of reference. Our knowledge and conditioning kicks in and decides for us.

The Organism eye does not have any cultural underpinning. It reacts from a much more simplistic and basic source. In a cinematic context, when it comes to appealing to the lowest common denominator, the Organism eye has huge currency. Steven Spielberg has managed to appeal to this very Organism eye through his movies—the *Jurassic Park* series, *E.T. the Extra-Terrestrial*, *Jaws*, and *A.I. Artificial Intelligence*—which did not necessarily require a cultural context to flow across borders.

Currently, what we see as a key component of Indian cinema—especially the Bollywood song-and-dance gamut—is a distinctive flavour, not an offering in its entirety. If Indian cinema needs to—for market realities—cater to the lowest common denominator, it can, and it can do so in far more interesting and innovative ways. For example, India has a penchant for the fantastical—the 'adbhut'—which is found in abundance in its literary wealth.

With growing technical expertise, it could be interesting to explore cinema through an Organism eye and create a unique cinematic spectacle in its own right. Perhaps, even a culturally embedded subject and mythological deity like Hanuman could be viewed from the 'Cultural eye' standpoint and also carry universal appeal as a hero from the 'Organism eye' perspective. Celebrating cinema as a medium of expression and leveraging it for reasons of commerce is a challenging undertaking. The issue one needs to constantly address is that cinema is not merely a reflection of society, but also shapes sensibilities. To be able to create indelible impressions that transcend and influence the collective consciousness of the society is no easy task but this is where the possibilities are richer, and I look forward to our cinema taking on this hue as well.

19

Romance in Hindi Cinema: Reverence and Realism in Film Songs

In a country where people read less and listen more—in keeping with our oral traditions—songs have kept philosophies, emotions and beliefs intact. They have reflected the morality of their times in a defined form. Marking journeys from the cradle to the grave, music and songs can be found in the nooks and crannies of India's existence. Its classical and folk traditions have been a treasure trove; an expression and song can be found for every occasion and sentiment. However, over the last hundred years or so, it's the songs on the celluloid which have impacted our psyche. I have often said that whilst the Indian film industry has been prolific in many a department, but lyrically, barring a few phases, it has been par excellence. The content of our songs, in many a case, can be effortlessly quoted like sheer poetry.

Actually, a study of our film song lyrics can be a crash course on the subject of the popular consciousness of India through the decades. At a glance though, one might come to the hurried conclusion that Indian people are overtly romantic, for romance has been the backbone of Indian film music and song. The truth, as it unfolds itself, is contrary. Over the years, the layers of the intricate social and moral fabric of the country have made a simple and natural man-woman relationship bear the burden of social restriction and sanction. I don't wish to get into which region(s), caste(s) or part(s) of society is more responsible for this, but the fear that romance had the power to break down the joint family system and the other sub-units of relationships was predominant.

The eagerness of the society to play a key role and the denial of a natural and beautiful relationship resulted in romance being more layered, complex, sacred and, paradoxically, beautiful. In this kind of a societal structure, the significance of love songs cannot be overstated.

Since romance was taboo, it was expressed through the medium of poetry and songs—whether it was to convey your feelings to the object of your affection (*'Mausam hai aashiqana'*; *'Tere hussn ki kya tareef karoon?'*) or self-expression ('*Meri aankhon se koi neend liye jata hai*'; '*Koi aaya dhadkan kehti hai*'; and '*Dheere dheere machal ae dil-e-beqarar*'). Many more facets were also expressed, such as:

- Desire: '*Door reh ke na karo baat, kareeb aajao*'; '*Mora gora ang leyi le*'.
- Intention: '*Mere dil mein aaj kya hai*'; '*Pyaar par bass toh nahi hai mera lekin*'.
- Playfulness: '*Hum aap ki aanhkon mein, iss dil ko basa de toh*'.
- Longing: '*Abhi na jao chhod kar*'; '*Yaad kiya dil ne*'; '*Hum bekhudi mein tumko pukare chale gaye*'.
- Togetherness: '*Tere mere sapne*'; '*Aap ki aankhon mein kuch mehke huye se raaz hai*'; '*Nain so nain*'.
- Grievance: '*Apni toh har aah bhi ek toofan hai*'.
- Pain and catharsis: '*Rasik balma, haaye dil kyon lagaya*'; '*Waqt ne kiya kya haseen sitam, tum rahe na tum, hum rahe na hum*'; '*Hui shaam unka khayal aagaya*'; '*Mann re tu kahe na dheer dhare*'; '*Hoke majboor mujhe usne bulaya hoga*'; '*Tere bina zindagi se koi shikwa to nahin*'.

> The content of our songs, in many a case, can be effortlessly quoted like sheer poetry.

In effect, physical appreciation, too, found its idiom through the transparent veil of the Hindi film song: *'Chhoo lene de nazuk honthon ko'*; *'Chandan sa badan'*; *'Chaudvin ka chaand ho'*. Most of the above couldn't be shown in scenes or said directly in dialogues. It would either be deemed irreverent or ridiculous. Class and taste had to be maintained, and the social codes of conduct which male-female relationships followed, had to be respected. So, much of the responsibility for articulation lay on songs. They not only moved the narrative forward but also added another dimension. It is undisputable that film songs were the best medium of conveying romance and passion in a society where onscreen permissiveness was taboo, till recently.

Perhaps that is the reason why our earlier songs resided in the space of longing and amplified pathos. The societal and physical distance was so much that probably, the first five times, the boy and girl were only able to glance at each other. The boy would then wait for weeks to even muster up the courage to cycle or drive past her house, and then wait for months before the first sentence was uttered. The longing and intensity built up gradually. In fact, often the very feeling of being in love surpassed the desire of union, because time and again, the conformist in a person led them to nurture the love for one, and tread a different part with another—society. In 99 per cent of the cases, love lost and society won.

Another factor which I feel underlines the language and tenor of songs of the early 1950s and, to some extent, '60s, was a fusion of Mughal aristocracy and elements of 'tehzeeb' (refinement), with that of brahmanical restraint. In hindsight, it was perhaps a bit patronizing. Tunes were heavily inspired from Hindustani classical music ragas and thumris, and voices were classically trained and refined. After all, music in itself—barring the common, folk variety—was initially the domain of a few.

Nurtured and patronized by the privileged, classical music was not for the masses but the select few. Songs held a mirror to a generation's and society's morality.

> Today, the repression, taboo and stigma associated with romance are considerably less; so is the enigma.

If the 1950s were about optimism and idealism, the '60s marked slight societal disillusionment and gentle romance. The newer generation of the '70s portrayed more overt romance and there was an erosion of the moral fabric in the '80s and '90s. After this, came a time when the voices of different social strata came into the limelight. Songs like 'Achha Sila Diya Tune Mere Pyaar Ka' or 'Tum To Thehere Pardesi' went on to become huge hits. From tune to lyrics to the kind of voices used, it marked the beginning of the common man's expression finding its place in the mainstream of Indian music.

This brings me to ponder over the romantic morality—if one can call it that—of the earlier decades and now. One key aspect, I observe, that has seen a definite decline, is the aspect of 'worshipping' the lover. Songs with lyrics like *'Prem jogan ban ke'* or *'Tumhi meri puja, tumhi devtaa ho'*, wherein the 'devotion' to the lover was very overt, have decreased. It is a factor of change in society. Earlier, physical and societal distance played a big role in creating an enigma and aura that was larger than life—often heavy with hyperbole.

Today, the repression, taboo and stigma associated with romance are considerably less; so is the enigma. The ethereal, unattainable and, therefore, venerated part of romance is now on the backburner. There is less symbolism and fewer metaphors. Many would argue that songs like 'Mann Ki Lagan' (*Paap*) or 'Tum Se Hi' (*Jab We Met*) are reminiscent of the melodious love songs of yore, that they strike more than a chord and transport you to a lighter space. I agree wholeheartedly, but not with the refrain that these songs are in the 'classic romance genre'—one that will live forever, the way the genre of classic love stories, such as 'Heer-Ranjha' or 'Romeo-Juliet', have. It's more like romantic nostalgia ('This is how romance used to/should be'), or the 'retro' kind of appeal that is reflected.

Today, romance has changed its expression. There are many possible reasons for this: The speed of our lives, the eroding morality of society, romance becoming disposable and temporary, increasingly fast-paced narrative of our cinema, lack of space for songs, etc.

I would take a slightly different view: I would say romance has found a different portrayal, a newer hue. Today, the man-woman relationship has evolved, societal conflict is comparatively less, and gender equations have changed. Today's woman doesn't want, or like, to be referred to as *'tyaag ki murti'* (epitome of sacrifice) or 'devi' (goddess)—the ever-sacrificing and suffering one. She is just another human—confident of living with both her flaws and strengths—and desirous of being accepted as just that. And I would say that, gradually, men are recognizing and echoing this aspect, and celebrating the new woman.

> *Today's woman doesn't want, or like, to be referred to as 'tyaag ki murti' or 'devi'...*

Romance is a gentler sentiment. It is what both elevates us and, paradoxically, sinks us into depths of emotion. Songs that portray love in all its beauty and complexity, and which carry with them the whiff of innocence and intensity of passion, will never fade. But perhaps, today, there is more realism in romance. There is a desire of not just romance but a romantic 'relationship'; that of a deeper understanding and experiencing a different shade of love: *'Rehna tu hai jaisa tu... thoda sa dard tu, thoda sukoon'.* Romance, as we knew it, is perhaps dead.

Long live romance!

SECTION 4

Hear It Echo

The heart of communication is in its decoding, or 'samphreshan', as it's called in Sanskrit. Being understood is desired by all creators of art forms. But pure art thrives on interpretation, openness and the space available to fill in our own self. There is always room for the receiver to conjure his or her own version through what they have consumed in a sensorial way.

That's why art is subjective, personalized and breathes very close to you, in rhythm with your beat. In communication, though art remains an important part, clarity becomes paramount. The precision of targeting your message and being able to deliver it sans fuzziness is critical. The thought, idea and meaning must be decoded; it must resonate and play back—literally echo. Calibrated fragrance, measured expression—the art of communication needs to find its space therein.

20

Art of Communication: Neurons, Gigabytes and Gaps

Over the last odd century, we have witnessed fundamental shifts, be it in political and economic systems or in our social context. Communication has perhaps seen the more significant of these changes. It was some hundred thousand years ago that speech transformed human communication; symbols and writing followed eventually to make us the mass connected civilization we are today. Analysing this from an academic perspective is perhaps not as compelling for me as much as exploring the impact I have personally and more palpably felt, both as a tech lover and a communication professional. There's an elemental change that the advent of technology has made, not just in the form but in the value of the ways that we express and connect. Here, we have seen massive alteration and, gaining connectivity and multiple modes of connection, have also lost several narratives.

A LOST NARRATIVE: MUSIC

As a teenager, for a few years I lived in Meerut, a small north Indian town. It was not easy to find music stores and, especially, one that stocked Hindustani classical music. It simply did not make business sense as there was low demand for classical music. However, being a music aficionado, I constantly sought it. If someone had recordings of the ragas rendered by Kumar Gandharva, it necessitated several rounds of requests, a trip down to buy a TDK cassette, the hunt for a resourceful person who owned a two-slot music system that had a recorder and a payment of a precious ₹5 to get him to copy it for me. The details carefully written down on the cover, the cassette became a small treasure. Many of my friends went through similar pangs with their choice of English songs or versions of Casey Kasem's 'Coast to Coast'. There is a certain memory and a kind of a narrative around that thirst and search.

Today, all I need is a credit card number and an Internet connection. Buying music is that simple. Perhaps, today, we overvalue the content. Content, in itself, has 'x' value. But layered with experience and narrative, it becomes a powerful and precious memory. Today, content is readily available but the narrative is rare. In fact, I sometimes deliberate whether, today, we listen to music for the love of it or simply as a memory device. More often some pieces of music—be they pure classical or folk—are not enjoyed in their pure form and have to be made palatable for 'popular listening'. As discussed earlier, words are oversimplified, and in some cases, dumbed down with emphasis, just to create a hook line.

Are we then dealing with conditioned minds that are culturally trained in one way or another? Is music, then, more of a reflex action—a habit? This is because, at times, reaction to music seems almost premeditated. The majority doesn't really buy music. They buy a block of emotions instead: 'Nostalgia', 'romantic', 'spurned in love', 'devotional', 'techno', 'party', 'dance'. A song is enjoyed not so much for its individual standing but as a part of the bigger package of music. Preconceived emotions surge up and numb us into enjoying a song that fits into a familiar mould. The creative construct of a song—the complexity of composition, depth of lyrics or the intricacies of instrumentation—are rarely paid any attention to. The criterion for judging music and songs seems to

> *I sometimes deliberate whether, today, we listen to music for the love of it or simply as a memory device?*

have been replaced by one all-encompassing quality—its 'entertainment' value. This is perhaps a reflection of our times where shallow, instant gratification is given more prominence than the weight of content.

A LOST NARRATIVE: BOOKS

Books were another important medium through which thoughts, points of view and emotions were communicated and continue to be—to a degree. We have our iPads and Kindles and an ease of access to virtual bookstores. Earlier, getting the book one wanted to read was not an easy task. It meant waiting for a friend or acquaintance to first finish reading, post which, the book would be borrowed and devoured, or it would entail a visit to the club or public library, where precious hours would be spent browsing, before coming across the couple of books one wanted to befriend over the next week or so. Again there was physicality (the hardbound cover, the feel and smell of paper)—a narrative around it. Friends were made, and sometimes broken up with, for the sake of a book given or not returned. Allow me to also examine the handy 'read later' function that we have today. I—and one suspects many—have clicked on the 'read later' button never to have really gotten around to actually doing so. There's a sense of procrastination; earlier, the perishable nature of the moment made one consume it better.

A LOST NARRATIVE: IMAGES

Today, my iPad has the latest books and scores of photographs, all of which reside in the mental comfort zone of existence, perhaps too conveniently so. The dilemma of buying the twenty-four- or thirty-six-picture reel is missing and so is perhaps the mindful weighing of making the thirty-six shots count, each of which was carefully composed and posed for. Now, a single shot is taken twenty to thirty times with a trigger-friendly digital camera and as easily discarded. The entire narrative around going to the shop and waiting for the reel to be washed and the prints and negatives handed and pored over excitedly in the shop itself, whilst fervently counting how many of the twenty-four or thirty-six were wasted, is no longer relevant. There are thousands of photographs in the hard drive memory today, but perhaps the value of the few we had earlier, was more. The purpose of the photographs, too, has changed. They triggered memories, transporting you to an incident in soft focus. Today, imagination itself has little place. The world has shrunk; it's the world of immediate reality. One rarely elucidates the experience of a place or incident, smartphones are browsed and the

> *From neurons, we have moved to gigabytes, converting biological memory into tech memory.*

picture shown 'right there' and then moved on with. The liminal space, where your and others' imagination found space to take form and breathe, is now too well defined. From neurons, we have moved to gigabytes, converting biological memory into tech memory.

Biological memory has a filter. It stores things with an emotional bias, because what adds significance is the emotion. This emotional bias comes in at the very fundamental stage of storage. For a tech memory, we do not have that. It's accessed through an easy, readymade window sans deep involvement. The narrative that the effort and imagination provided, stands somewhat diluted.

A LOST NARRATIVE: KNOWLEDGE

This aspect reflects in the manner in which knowledge is getting redefined in this information age. It's now democratized and accessible to all. It's wonderful that there is a free flow of information at a mass level but perhaps the ease of access makes it less special in some respects. Today, a dinner table conversation is not illuminated by the person who instinctively quotes from a poem, a couplet of Ghalib's or reels off a mind-boggling statistic, stored away considerately and passionately in their memory and heart, where it lived and breathed. Anyone on the table can google instantly to complete the couplet or present additional bits and bytes. Things are hurriedly scanned through and rarely pondered over. From a blotting paper, our minds are turning into smooth plastic where absorption is less and fewer things penetrate through the surface—a loss of a kind; for only that which is internalized can truly impact and transform. Knowledge stored with a narrative is deliciously warm; accessing it only through technology makes it a trifle cold.

> *Every new age brings its own narrative, but let not the charm and bittersweet pang of nuance be forgotten.*

A LOST NARRATIVE: LANGUAGE

The language in which this information and knowledge is received and communicated, too, has been altered. Language had to be learnt and adhered to, but today, language is subservient; it can be moulded very easily. We have witnessed the 'chutneyfying' of English, for example, Hindi and Tamil phrases have been mixed with those of English to bring in a 'Hinglish' or 'Tamglish' flavour. Even the Internet, which has been around only about twenty-five odd years, has been adding online language codes of emoticons and abbreviations. Be it in everyday parlance, official communication, social media or mass media entertainers, a liberal dose of intermingling is far more pronounced. It is a fact that language has to evolve, but the delicate fibre of an authentic language and a unique dialect needs some protection as well. The Kumaoni language, for example, has some twenty odd words to describe particular kinds of smell. Today, only a few remain in use. Take, the Galo language of Arunachal Pradesh, which reportedly has a uniquely encoded grammar that refrains one from assuming and referring to a third person's thoughts—this, too, is on the wane. This is regrettable, for a word is a capsule of culture; along with the dying of a language, its folklore, rituals, customs and learnings, too, asphyxiate.

Over the years, a shift towards the homogenization of language has simultaneously led to the watering down of the precious heritage and intellectual legacy of varied mini cultures. Rising individualism, too, has played a role in the way communication has changed form. Self-expression is fundamental and remains so, but the desire to own, consume and micro-express for the self has gained more traction in the last few decades. This has been, of course, linked deeply to the advent and popularity of social media platforms.

AGE OF INSTANT COMMUNICATION

Granted that social media has made communication easier and faster, made people more connected and has presented unheard of opportunities, but it has its limitations as well. I recall a few years ago, an online platform called 'Second Life'—the virtual world which was cited as the next big thing. Different identities were assumed and a life was led online. But as I donned an avatar on Second Life, what struck me even then, was that the codes followed were not new or unique. The pursuit of finding a mate, buying property, opening an office, fashioning a wedding, planning a funeral—all were borrowed from the real world.

However, one aspect where I reckon communication and expression have taken on another hue, is that of anonymity. Not that it didn't exist earlier but perhaps, anonymity was not so rampant. Today, in the comfort of online anonymity, any deviant can much more easily find resonance, be it a political ideology or sexual behaviour. Anonymity provides the comfort to communicate without a social identity.

Of course, the bright side of instant communication, especially for social good—be it protests or playing a seminal 'viral' role in revolutions like in the Arab spring—is laudable. However, we mustn't forget that it's not only the medium but also the power of an idea that's at play; for it's the power of idea or the power of emotion that gets communicated, virally or otherwise. The art of communication, and its methodology and tools have indeed changed dramatically over the last odd century and we are in a state of flux, where these will take their time to settle and evolve.

Every new age brings its own narrative, but let not the charm and bittersweet pang of nuance be forgotten. Let's definitely celebrate the new and the better, but more importantly, let's not lose the ability to pause, to listen to the murmurs and lament what is worth lamenting. After all, the past and the present together morph into the tomorrows.

21

When Will Indian Advertising Go Global?

There is much talk of 'global and local', especially when it comes to the Indian advertising industry. It is now facing newer challenges as well as opportunities when it comes to their portfolio of, on one hand, established multinational brands which want to further explore the Indian market, and on the other, emerging local brands which harbour global ambitions. And in this context, there is also pressure on Indian advertising to find its place on the world stage and be part of the so-called 'global culture'.

However, let us first examine why there is a need or

desire of going global, especially from an advertising and creative perspective:

- Is it to beget global awards and recognition?
- Is it about connecting with a larger customer base?
- Is it to test whether homegrown ideas and concepts can make the world sit up and take note?
- Is it about the world needing global ideas?
- Is it about a sense of 'Indianness' appealing to the world, or India being able to blend into the world dynamics?

In the midst of this debate, let us not lose sight of the fact that advertising is closely related to the cultural context of the market it operates in; for, in order to connect with the consumer base, the social milieu is of immense importance.

Advertising, in this context, is viewed as a universal cultural signifier of commercialism. Does it then imply that for Indian advertising to succeed on the world stage, our indigenous social and cultural context will have to let a more uniform global culture take precedence?

In my view, there are variables at play and the answer may lie in all of these and maybe a few more; for, even though many of us believe that we are moving towards globalization—hence, standardization—I feel that it is not so simplistic. The juxtaposition of various cultures is bound to result into a more complex society. The cross-cultural fertilization will sprout another hybrid, which would be even more different and layered at first, for us to understand.

For advertising to be globally effective in this context, I believe that it is not an 'outside in', but an 'inside out' approach that is going to be more productive. Therefore, before we embark on attempting to take the local onto a global platform, it is important to understand more lucidly what is happening locally.

India has been—and is—a complex market. Often within our country, products, communication and advertising have to be tweaked and tailor-made for different regions. What may work in the South may not necessarily apply in the same form in the North or East. And apart from the multifarious regional sensibilities, even on a macro level, there is an increasing need to 'understand and connect with the "changing" Indian consumer'.

By the time you read through the books, theories and researches on consumer behaviour, the consumer seems to have moved on. Not that the Indian consumer had not gone through change earlier; but this time, the speed at which he/she is changing is more important. The new consumer who is emerging, is embracing and confidently exhibiting this

> *For advertising to be globally effective in this context...it is not an 'outside in', but an 'inside out', approach that is going to be more productive.*

change. It is a consumer who will not necessarily enjoy when you talk to him/her in his/her own dialect but a consumer who would say, 'You speak the way you do; I will speak my way. And let's talk'. It is a more confident consumer.

There is no longer the leeway to take a higher ground and talk down or show a way up. The need for communication that talks more eye to eye and one to one, is stronger than before. This understanding really helped me a lot in my creations, in advertising. I believe the work done on Fevicol, Coca-Cola or Happydent—which were applauded on international platforms like Cannes, Clio and D&AD—have kept true to our local ethos.

A myth that the famous '*Thanda matlab...*' ad campaign successfully managed to break was that the Indian youth could be reached only through lifestyle advertising. It was equally popular with both the trendy urban and the curious rural youth. This made it clear that the Indian youth was not necessarily rebellious. He/she was confident of successfully creating a world which will be able to contain both—his/her desire as well as tradition.

At the same time, I feel we must recognize the fact that as a society we are still in the 'pupa' stage, undergoing transformation. Our society today is much more fluid and not likely to settle soon into one standard identifiable entity. The relevance of retaining and drawing inspiration from local ethos comes from the fact that standardization needs to be bypassed and innovative and fresh thinking brought in.

It is the local flavour that lends a fresh perspective. And in the race for globalization, we must not leave our local sensibilities behind, for this will ensure that we retain our distinctive edge. But what is this local flavour? Showing and utilizing the oft-repeated images—in the case of India, the land of spiritual gurus, yoga and elephant rides; China as the land of Kung Fu; or Africa as that of wildlife and Zulu dancers? I think not.

A genuine local flavour comes from not just the visual reality but by understanding the social psyche. These, in turn, come from the existence around us. One has to soak in the varied experiences; for then, what you squeeze out on paper or celluloid will be original, refreshing and unique. For instance, let's look at two inimitable aspects of local culture in India, which when used to portray the country on a global stage, can make us stand apart.

> *Genuine local flavours come not from just the visual reality but by understanding the social psyche.*

ART OF CHAOS AND CONTRADICTION

If the West is about minimalistic linearity, India is a country of layers, of chaos. Take music for instance. Western notes are staccato; in Indian music, you will keep coming back to the 'sthayi' (the initial phrase of a composition). It's cyclic. Take our typical Indian weddings for example—there are numerous ceremonies and rituals that seem to go on simultaneously. Everyone in the family has a role to play and are extremely busy with an endless list of things to do. In the midst of all this, often the bride and the groom are incidental and there are numerous other focal points.

Compare that to an orderly western scenario where, more often than not, there are 'wedding rehearsals' that take place and it is an event planned and run by the bride and groom. From that perspective, our Indian weddings may seem chaotic.

Talking of contradictions, consider our roads: You will find both the latest, swanky model of a car and the old model of a scooter. The same country that boasts of the cream of Information Technology is still fighting illiteracy. These are but some observations on how easily extremes exist in India. But there is a bit of magic and charm in this very Indian phenomenon of a coexistence with chaos. There is a unique method to this madness. And when we choose to leverage that, we succeed in carving a niche for ourselves.

Take, for example, the Indian film industry. Rather than adhering to international norms, we have our very own take. Our films are not about 'what' but about 'how'. The stories are, willy-nilly, the same. And before we enter the cinema hall, we often know that the hero and heroine will fall in love, there will be songs, some melodrama, a villain, some comic scenes and, in the end, the good guys will triumph. But still we sit and watch the film. Why? Because we love to see the 'how'. It is like watching a boxing match vis-à-vis a WWE match. In the former, you don't know what and how it is going to happen; in the latter you do, but you still watch it because you *enjoy* how it is going to happen.

Today, even the Bollywood style of song and dance belongs as much on the global stage as it does in India. And rather than ignoring this or trying to ape global sensibilities, if we learn to showcase this very chaos in our communication and advertising, our work will be distinctive.

THE ORAL TRADITION

India is a country with a strong oral tradition—another distinctive local Indian convention. We are an audio-led country. For generations, literature, poetry and local wisdom was passed on and imbibed, orally. Kabir, one of our famed saint-poets, was not familiar with the written word and yet his poetry lived because it was recited through generations. Even our great epics, like *Ramayana*, are written in metre and not prose. I can't think of another country that has so many structures of metre available. Our ancient words of wisdom—'dohas' or 'chaupais'—were also written in metre to make them easier to remember.

Recitation and listening have lived on in India. Even at a small-town teashop, you will find one man reading aloud an item from the newspaper while the others listen on. It is not that the rest cannot read or cannot afford that newspaper; it is the innate trait of being used to the oral tradition. Spoken words have a unique hold over us. We, as a country, *remember* words and dialogues, and quote them.

If we understand and leverage this in our communication, the consumer connect will be stronger. For example, I have often said that the power of radio is underutilized in our communication to the masses. We should exploit this bent towards the oral tradition. If a radio communication is written well and implemented properly, it is likely to meet with instant acceptance.

We have to play from these areas of our strengths and not bypass them in order to make our offering more easily acceptable. Hence, our advertising, instead of going the way the rest of the world does (with minimal words or clever one-liners), could exploit this very Indian penchant for the spoken word and overt expression, and manage to stand apart.

If we apply the same understanding on a larger global platform, we will find that the cultural nuances that are part of our ethos resonate equally in most parts of the world, especially Asia, which is such a varied mix of races, cultures and traditions.

VARYING EXPRESSION; SAME EMOTION

I am reminded of an interesting experience, some time back. I was visiting one of the South East Asian countries, the creative responsibility of which I bear, and met with one of my local directors. Extending his hospitality, he invited me to a restaurant serving authentic local food. In the midst of our meal and conversation, he turned a trifle sentimental. The food reminded him of the meals cooked by his grandmother.

He went on to relate how she roasted cockroaches and fed them lovingly, one at a time, to him and his eager cousins. To me, the idea of eating roasted cockroaches—obviously a delicacy in his part of the world—was strange. It was difficult for me to be on the same wavelength, for the gentleman was emotional about the incident and had a film of tears over his eyes. It then dawned on me emphatically: Replace the cockroaches with ladoos, and many of us will have similar stories of food and affection from our childhood.

> *We have to ensure that the uniqueness of our culture and its ethos is not compromised but leveraged.*

You see, the expression may vary but the emotion is the same. A grandmother's love is as endearing in China as it is in India or Norway.

For advertising or communication to be on a world stage and connect with consumers, what one has to unearth and be sensitive towards are intrinsic human emotions and insights.

No doubt, given the evolving consumer and changing social scenario, the task to reach out and communicate effectively is a complex one. But this is what makes advertising and communication an exciting business to be in. The quest is to unearth that one universal insight, come up with that one brilliant idea that transcends all differences, and clothe it in a relevant cultural context that then goes on to not just strike a chord but make your brand the preferred one. Herein, lies the challenge and the opportunity.

And whilst it is wonderful to get recognized internationally, to do so at the cost of overlooking our cultural context or 'oversimplifying' it, will be a recipe for disaster. We have to ensure that the uniqueness of our culture and its ethos is not compromised but leveraged.

22

Unreal World of Advertising!

In today's society, an aspect that seems to be waning is the ability to laugh at ourselves. Fortunately, as the advertising industry still has the leeway to view things in a lighter vein, let's use that lens for a while. Advertising commercials have a unique way of creating their own little world. And in this world, you find things that you rarely ever see, people you rarely ever meet, places you rarely ever go to. Let's check out a few of these 'ad only' things.

Repeat a lie a hundred times and it will become the truth, it is said. We, in advertising, have a slightly different take. We repeat something so many times that it dissipates. *'Doodh si safedi'* (Milk-like whiteness) must have been a great analogy when first used decades ago. But now, after being used ad nauseam, the metaphor stops being reflected—it starts reflecting the product. The creators may be happy that it gets associated strongly with the product, but the fact is, the benchmark itself has disappeared from the consumers' minds.

Another such favourite is *'Kya lajawaab swaad'* (What unmatchable taste). How many of us say this in real life when we eat something delicious? We might only say *'mazza aa gaya'* (this was really enjoyable), or just reach out for some more of the food.

Take the use of superlatives such as 'new' or 'best'. The client feels he has 'said it all', but is the consumer decoding them? More importantly, does the consumer believe in these claims? Advertising, in trying to create hyperbole, has sounded the death knell of superlatives. We have managed to make them irrelevant in the consumer's mind.

UNREAL WORLD

Take a look at some of the favourite characters you will find in the ad world. The 'cute' old people, always supercharged and super charming, are far removed from their sometimes non-communicative, cantankerous counterparts in the real world. If the product they are advertising, is for vitality, you can buy the 'super oldies' formula'. But not for all! In real life, I have yet to come across the robust, turbo-charged and chirpy senior citizens shown in our ads, irrespective of the product being endorsed.

A mother-in-law in an ad film will perennially be an over-critical one, and the household help, a garrulous, intrusive character that we would probably never tolerate in real life. We excel at simplifying complex humans into one type, regardless of age, class, caste and creed. They have no existence outside the world, but in this world, they live king size.

Also, all kinds of things talk—cockroaches, mosquitoes, the vegetables in the kitchen, the cooking oil... Sometimes, even a chicken merrily tells the world what a delicious meal it will make! Ice cubes dance, and people in ancestral photographs—sepia-coloured but full of life—rotate their eyes, twirl their moustaches and smile coyly.

> *In the hope of becoming aspirational, we often make the mistake of alienating the consumer.*

In the advertising world, the language, people and situations often don't mirror society. In the hope of becoming aspirational, we often make the mistake of alienating the consumer.

REAL WORKS

Clients and creators need to understand that there is nothing more amazing—and relatable—as real life. Very few examples come to mind when you think of ads that score on real-life situations or people. A leading newspaper's campaign, where a retired man tries to push his pension file through a government office is a brilliant example. The situation, the setting, the acting and the running commentary-style narration makes a tremendous impact.

When an ad film for a soft drink brand shows a dialogue between a pretty girl and a shopkeeper revolving around the use of the word 'bhaiya', a lot of young men in small towns can relate to it: A situation when they have been branded 'brother-like' by the girl they were hoping to get romantically involved with.

There will be more such examples but, unfortunately, not many will wipe out the often overtly exaggerated images that we end up creating in advertising. We must draw inspiration from life around us and not get trapped into stereotypes and a make-believe world.

Suspending reason works well for the film industry because their product is often meant for entertainment. For us in the communication business, entertainment is a means to sell a product. And we can sell in the most effective manner if we are able to connect with our consumers in their own world and not perennially in some world of fantasy.

23

Advertising: Allure and Accountability

Questions about the role of advertising have always garnered much attention, be it pertaining to the key role in influencing political outcomes or the stakes of movie/sports icons' association with a product.

Advertising is something very fundamental to nature's way of existence and survival. Its roots can be found in the basic act of enticing another with what one has to offer. An exuberant display of this art can be found in the natural world—be it a peacock colourfully fluttering its intent or a frog using its vocal calisthenics, to attract attention. The phrase 'Dadur Kanthi', used in Hindustani classical music to describe a certain kind of voice quality meant for singing, probably comes from here.

But this aside, the point is: It would be unnatural to expect someone to start listing their shortcomings and start sharing those with the world. To display the best side and attract attention is natural. One will use what one has in his/her weaponry of lure.

Extending this to a product, a service or an idea, you would want the world to know what you are presenting is exceptional. There is nothing deviant about believing your offering to be unique. Out of a concrete product, you try to carve out an intangible, intricate brand. You are restless until there's a distance between what you believe is a unique offering and what the world thinks of it. But how do you bridge this gap, when you are not the only one who has this belief? Isn't it only fair that everyone feels the same way about their product?

So, 'the enticement parade' starts. Art is called for; persuasion gets in. Creativity gets employed and outsourced. This is where it is no longer natural. A peacock doesn't outsource the art of wooing. In nature, it is a rhythmic extension of the self, a manifestation of your desire to be accepted. It's not borrowed. In nature, your advertising is *you*. You become your ad; no confusion there.

So, is advertising in its current form not ideal for designing a brand and carving out a brand personality? No, that would be an overstatement.

It would be a natural progression if a product organically grows into a brand and tiptoes into the subconscious, residing alongside human emotions. But the wait for the stages in between is long, and impatience sets in. Evolution is a gradual process and you want to grow your product into a brand in your lifetime, not in Darwinian time. Hence, some tools are deployed, which will help you reach out to the world. These tools keep evolving as human civilizations evolve.

Ages ago, one used a whistle for a dog. One still does, and the dog is influenced as it was hundreds of years back. The human mind though is exploring, imagining and expanding its horizons, and is no longer excited by old creative whistles. You have to keep evolving the ways of arresting attention. So you sing, dance, speak, animate, hire celebrities. You borrow anything which may help you communicate your belief about what you are offering.

> *No one frowns at advertising; it's accepted as part of the orchestra called consumerism.*

This moves along fine till you operate from a true belief. In the consumerist world we live in today, the art of building a brand through creativity is well understood, at least by a significant section of our society. No one frowns at advertising; it's accepted as part of the orchestra called consumerism. In fact, you almost can't imagine this music without it.

But what if there is no belief to begin with and there is only greed for disproportionate profit? What if there is no intention to express your brand; there is no restlessness for bridging the proverbial gap; and it's just lust for profit—adulterated lust—sans any responsibility and at any cost? This marks the entry of manipulation in what is simply a naturally competitive world.

The reasons to lure, then, become different and dishonest in the core. Hence, the means deployed will be more perfidious. Nobody expects that a product or brand will be solely for altruistic reasons—that would be expecting too much. But purity of intent, of a desire to share your uniqueness, is missing here.

This is the very scenario we need to guard ourselves against. This is where some vigilance is required. This is where checks and balances need to kick in—especially when art and creativity are in the fray. Employed creativity is rarely subtle. It goes all guns blazing, and is more lethal and focused.

Celebrity endorsement, in normal course, has little to be concerned about, but in the twisted scenario, where the intention is adulterated, there are filters required. The question about who should bear the brunt would be intricate to answer as the structure has many shareholders. However, one thing is certain: The consumer needs to be protected, at any cost, from profiteering.

I've believed that the ideal world, in a mystical way, creates natural checks and balances. Human conscience holds supreme and collectively guides towards the better. But sometimes, it has to be actively steered to stay the course. A dancing peacock not only delights the target audience but becomes a symbol of enduring beauty for many others—from a vision that is beautifully etched, to the dropped feather safely ensconced in a favourite book. As long as the intent is natural and not a corrupted one, advertising will continue to be a wonderful platform to amplify unique voices.

24

Promotions in an Indian Context

Just like advertising, the effectiveness of promotions has also been questioned in the Indian context by statements like 'Promotions do not work'. The common refrain is that they do not work because consumers claim that their buying decision is based chiefly on the quality of the main product and the freebies are of no consequence.

Most marketers would take this with more than a pinch of salt and give facts and figures on the efficacy of a planned strategy for increasing sales over a short period. After all, it's commonly held that promotions add value to the product or service offered, and stimulate sales for reasons other than the product's inherent benefits. Those reasons, they would decree, are 'incentives', and they work because 'people like something for nothing'. Why, then, is there a seeming anomaly between customer talk and behaviour?

I believe that promotions can be beneficial for the brand and have many merits but to be overtly acknowledged as 'the reason' to buy or consume, they must be in sync with not only the brand values but the consumer's social context as well. After all, promotions come from life itself. Let me share an example with you. The summer holidays of my childhood were spent in the hills of Almora. At dusk, a respected, elderly gentleman called aloud from his house atop the hill: 'C'mon kids, time for the evening session.' All the children, including me, would eagerly run up to his tiny mountain abode, where, for the next hour or so, we enthusiastically sung traditional songs in the local dialect. As kids, the magnet was the sweet offerings that he distributed at the end of the hour. We got ladoos, fruits, and sometimes, even freshly made halwa.

> *If the product is not good enough, the promotions will kill a brand faster than anything else.*

The offering, in a way, for us kids, was the 'promotion' for the 'product': The value system that he sought to inculcate, and the cultural and traditional ethos he wanted us to experience and be part of. Though not in the context of this example, but in all likelihood, the fact is that the allure of something extra cuts across all age and income groups. People, however, hesitate to accept it as thus. They seldom admit it openly; perhaps, not even to themselves.

But why? I guess we need to contextualize this closet consumption of promotions in terms of our social ethos. Greed is, perhaps, universally frowned upon but it may be opposed a little more than usual, in our milieu. Some may argue otherwise, but we do have a deeply embedded cultural value system that places emphasis on frugality and 'santosh' (contentment). The 'extra for self' or the overt 'want for more than necessary' is considered crass. For promos, too, paradoxically, the freebie is readily accepted, if couched in a deeper reason to buy the main product. It, therefore, would work better to ensure that the promos and offers are crafted carefully—be it for a product or a programme concept. They should be in sync with, and not contradictory to, the brand values we seek to build or a social context which is acceptable. It would be incongruous to offer a free chocolate with a pack of toothpaste, or potato chips with chawanprash.

We also need to remember that promos do not work for a bad product. If you expect it to do a 'saviour's' job, it will not succeed. If the product is not good enough, the promotions will kill a brand faster than anything else. But, if done in sync with the brand values and, additionally, the social context, they can definitely enhance the appeal of a product. Perhaps that is why, though I have long forgotten the taste of the sweets, I still, on occasion, find the traditional songs echoing, because they, in themselves, were extraordinary.

25

Women in Indian Ads: From Selling Products to Leading Change

Advertising and marketing have frequently engaged women to sell products, not only in terms of models but also as a means to reach more households. But have brands and communication in India, specifically targeted women *as* individuals? Have marketers specifically designed products keeping women in mind?

Barring a few clichéd exceptions in obvious categories, like that of feminine hygiene, one can contend that this has not been the case. And the reason cannot be just the lack of economic empowerment, for that could be the case for kids as well, who, despite this, are a direct and overt target audience for many products, and there is marketing communication targeted directly at the eleven to fourteen age group.

Is the Indian woman recognized as a serious consumer and decision-maker at all? Yes—if we view her in her designated roles, and perhaps, not when the question is that of acknowledging her as an individual entity. But before we start blaming marketers and advertisers, we need to understand the socio-traditional circumstances of women.

GLORIFYING SACRIFICE

An Indian woman and her institutionalized, societal situation—to my mind, at least—are intriguingly complex. In my view, unfortunately, a woman has still not been recognized as a complete individual. Traditionally, society has been in a hurry to push her into roles: The ideal daughter, the perfect wife, the dutiful daughter-in-law and the loving mother.

> *Even in advertising, it is the 'role-playing' woman—wife, loving mother, dutiful daughter-in-law—who is acknowledged.*

The transition from daughter to wife is acknowledged and encouraged because she typifies roles, but the phase between the two—where she is a lover—or a person who has decided to buck the trend of marriage and carve out a career for herself, are far from celebrated. At the one stage where she is being herself—just a woman, an individual person—she is allowed little space. Her awareness as an individual, her potential and self-expression in all dimensions—sexual or otherwise—is left unnurtured, buried under norms.

So, even in advertising, it is the 'role-playing' woman—wife, loving mother, dutiful daughter-in-law—who is acknowledged. Her 'sacrificial' role is venerated in society and advertising pays obeisance, so much so that, as marketers and communication experts, we cannot even sell to her the products or services on the convenience platform.

All the things that make her life easier—be it a washing machine or ready-made food—have to be sold not as products that will free her from the mundane, but couched in various benefits for her family.

The 'sacrifice' of self by a woman has been glorified. If asked to be honest and respond without the apprehension of being judged as a mother or wife, she'd probably admit that she would like to take advantage of products and appliances that make her chores easier. But meetings after meetings I have sat in, where research findings present that women don't want the 'pain' that they take for their families, they themselves are taken away from the equation, possibly because of a fear of losing relevance in a patriarchal setup.

Hypocritical? Of course! She is trapped in a societal framework that perpetuates these double standards. Society has pushed her to believe that making round chappatis is the best thing she could do and the communication machinery excels in propagating a fake sense of fulfilment for the inconsequential.

'Oh, you washer of the whitest shirts; the vanquisher of the cockroach; the one who can make a toilet seat sparkle; the mighty warrior who has defeated stubborn stains... we bow to you.'

Isn't this simply ridiculous?

As a society, these things have got credence because, somewhere, there is a traditional, subversive machinery at play, which works overtime to stop women from getting involved in the meaningful battles of life, the real decisive matters.

> *Partly driven by need and partly by opportunity, the woman's world is changing and, in turn, she is changing the world.*

SHE, LEADING THE CHANGE

Society has pushed and manipulated women into thinking that ultimate fulfilment lies in the mundane tasks of life, and worse, not acknowledged her as an individual entity and pushed her into typified roles.

It is not to say that a woman doesn't enjoy or take pride in cooking, maintaining a spotless home or being appreciated if her children look and perform to the best of their abilities. However, to glorify these as the only things that signify her worth, is patronizing. There is more that defines her.

Fortunately, it is increasingly evident that she is learning to decipher between real achievements and manufactured ones, and knows that her identity is dependent on the independence of her thoughts, intellect and compassion as an individual entity.

It is a no-brainer that it is education and economic freedom which have led to this growing awareness about her individuality and identity. In turn, she has started to expect more than just the basics from her partner and the social system around her; not in a materialistic sense of the word but on the parameters of empathy, respect, support, partnership—and sexuality.

There is an overall shift. Sexuality, from being owned by society, is being reclaimed through individuality. This is, perhaps, more visible in the metros today and hopefully, will have a trickle-down effect.

Interestingly, it is the Indian woman who is driving this change. Partly driven by need and partly by opportunity, the woman's world is changing, and in turn, she is changing the world. There are talks about men changing and becoming more accommodative as well as sensitive. To my mind, this is but a reaction. There is no option.

Faced with the power of the woman, men have to change.

Sure, we are in a transition phase and things are not going to settle down into one standard identifiable entity soon enough. But change there is. In these circumstances, we could do more than pay lip service to women—not just from a larger ethical point of view, but also that as a target audience. This is because there is a huge section of society waiting to be tapped—that of the individual female consumer. The marketing gaze will need to shift. This shift will gain momentum as more and more female marketers, brand managers, creative directors, scriptwriters and technicians make their way into the bastions that were dominated by a single gender with a singular lens.

As a society and industry, we will expand, excel and stand more enriched.

26
Rituals: A Powerful Brand Asset

Some time ago, while travelling, I savoured my few hours of suspension from reality, reclined my seat and selected a movie to play. A few minutes later, I was pleasantly surprised to see the purser walk up with a bag of popcorn. Who said you cannot have pasta or an omelette whilst watching a film? Why is it that only popcorn seems to hit the spot? Why does its smell enhance the feel of the film?

The truth is that it is a ritual which has been a part of our movie-going experience. A film seems incomplete without it.

It set me thinking: Are we creating less of such rituals in our lives and in our brands—be it in religion, where the often-heard refrain is 'I am not ritualistic', or in our brand world, where it's nearly absent, save a few that we still remember? A toothpaste brand created the breath ritual of 'Ha-Ha'; a chocolate brand created a ritual of breaking the wafers into two halves; and a beer brand created the 'slice of lime in the bottle spout' ritual. (There are many theories about the latter, ranging from it being a Mexican habit; to that of it being created by a Californian bartender for a lark, just to see how long it would take for a random new drinking ritual to catch on; and of construction workers and their practical idea of inserting a sliver of lime in the spout of the bottle to stop the dirt at the site from getting inside.)

Some rituals become synonymous with the product: A birthday cake is almost unthinkable without the customary candle ritual; the celebratory ritual of popping of the champagne bottle; in the old days, the ritual of shaking a Polaroid photo until it dried; and closer home, for many, that of dipping a glucose biscuit in tea.

Sure, it could be debated whether some of the above are examples of rituals or mere accompaniments. But instead of 'add-ons', I'd call them a unique property which enhances

> *Over a period of time, these layers enhance the product. People don't merely consume products; they also consume memories.*

consumption. I would reckon that something that elevates a product from the facet of mere functionality and adds an emotional value to it—by giving it a layered experience—is a ritual. Actual consumption is a very simple and direct process. Sex, in itself, is a pretty basic act, but the rituals created around it—the wooing, clothes, food, certain kind of music, lighting—add to its experience.

It is true that with the commoditization of brands and the homogenization of value propositions, brands need to create deep and meaningful bonds. These, in turn, generate loyalty that goes a long way in building business profitability and brand relationships. After all, bonds and associations with products are omnipresent in our daily lives.

Many of us may fondly remember the '*Khichri ke chaar yaar: dahi, papad, ghee, achaar*' practice. This way, a basic, mundane mish-mash of a dish is elevated to a meal which we love. To have it any other way may tinker with the taste, but also alters the entire experience. It's the little ritual of having these four side dishes that completes the experience of having the meal. The human orientation for aesthetics comes into play here. We do not want to accept that we are doing a 'basic' thing such as gulping food. We need to set ourselves apart from a primal desire of hunger. We do not want to accept the bare, stripped stuff; there is a desire to not feel animalistic, but artistic. A four-course meal, art of garnishing... they are all attempts to attach layers and meanings to basic acts of necessities.

Over a period of time, these layers enhance the product. People don't merely consume products; they also consume memories. *'Maa ke haath ka khana'* (home-cooked food) may have more to do with the memory of the happy times and the warmth of love, than with the taste. Probably, if you were to have a competition of 'meals cooked by moms', your mother's dish may be in the bottom lot. But then, actually the food is not the reason why you cherish it. Those small family rituals around the table—perhaps the grandmother feeding you the first bite; you swiping the hot chappati from your sibling; or your mother loading your plate to the brim—may have disappeared as you grew older, but it's those very spontaneous rituals which enhanced the taste of that food. Later in life, when you crave the same dish, it's more about revisiting that experience and recreating that magic.

> *Creating a ritual around a product or service takes time, but can become a powerful asset to a brand.*

In a similar vein, 'Hotel California', the title track from the album of the same name by The Eagles, is not so much to do with the song and composition, as it is with the experience of hostel and graduate life. Music, for many, is a memory-transportation device. It reminds one of a cherished experience. Rituals allow one to operate in this space. They go beyond habits and routines to create a deeper bond and become an integral part of people's lives. They create an enriched experience in a unique way that only a particular brand can provide.

Creating a ritual around a product or service takes time, but can become a powerful asset to a brand. However, it's essential that they are carefully crafted. If they have to become a seamless part, then they have to be simple—from real life. Rituals should not be generated in the boardroom, but by observing and understanding people's behaviour.

Lately, we seem to be creating more of the former. Certain so-called brand rituals—of kids chanting three nonsensical words, or doing a headstand before drinking their milk—is of the former kind which will have a short-lived life and not go too far. Many times, as advertisers, we confuse memory hooks with rituals. Rituals should be inspired from consumer behaviour, not a figment of one's imagination. Only then will the ritual make the experience more elaborate, more intricate and will find more takers.

While I munched on the popcorn, the opportunity and need to work harder to recognize and recreate the magical, warm practices called rituals, hit home stronger.

27
Subliminal Messaging: An Underused Tool

Big data, machine learning and AI have increasingly become part of brand strategies for communication with the consumer. Market segmentation, psychographics and demographics were all means to correctly identify and pitch the message to the audience. These have now been augmented with the availability of data—often in real time—giving birth to an era where 'targeting' has found a new meaning.

'Precision'—the sharpness with which one can target the consumer and reach at a juncture when he/she is more likely to consume the message favourably, and moreover, act upon it—is holy grail today. Marketers are continually learning from user behaviour and customizing their pitch to optimize sales. The case of an irate father threatening to sue a departmental store is now part of advertising/data industry folklore. The father, seething with rage, presented the messages addressed to his school-going daughter—still in her teens—about product offers for maternity clothing, baby products and pictures of smiling infants. Furious and indignant, he chided the store personnel about this inappropriate messaging. The manager apologized, and a few days later, called to have a senior to express regret again. The father then sheepishly admitted that he had just come to know that his teenage daughter was pregnant. The departmental store's data analytics algorithm had figured, based on buying behaviour patterns, what a close family member may only get to know much later. This intersection of data and human behaviour has opened up new possibilities—that of predicting what one wants, even before they know that they want them.

Analytics and machine learning are laying out a new hypertargeting dynamic. For example, OTT (over the top) or digital streaming platforms aren't merely taking into account what the subscriber has watched or rated, but also what kind of content is being watched multiple times and which portions are being skipped. These patterns, when analysed and correlated, help to sharply target and match content with consumer.

Other companies have found ways to turn specific sets of information into specific articles for readers, which are sometimes indistinguishable from those written by human beings. Companies across the spectrum, from hospitality to cosmetics, are increasingly using 'chat bots'. The analysis of our needs—the mundane, material, and now, even the finer ones—are outsourced. It is not far-fetched to say that soon AI will be able to correlate different pieces to create consumption occasions.

Ponder over this scenario-creation for a while: A weather app figures that it's going to be a cool Friday evening with a slight drizzle; the calendar sync shows that you don't have any plans for that evening; an app consulting your playlist figures your music choice for that evening; and the messaging app forms a message, inviting friends over for an impromptu evening of monsoon snacks—hot pakoras and tea. '*Rasm-e-duniya bhi hai, mauka bhi, dastoor bhi hai*' gets a new spin; for, all these suggestions are not really man-made, but coming from technology. It sounds very convincing to say that when such targeting is done, it's going to be more result-oriented, as chances are that the mood for consumption is preempted.

> *The analysis of our needs–the mundane, material, and now, even the finer ones– are outsourced.*

Let me broaden the lens a little and touch upon another aspect: Marketing and advertising's age-old and oft-repeated phrase is: 'A good salesman can sell a refrigerator to an Eskimo.' It refers to the power of persuasion, the art of selling and the belief that the latter can create desires or make the customer inclined to what is being sold. Hidden somewhere in this adage, is the belief that people don't buy for the simple satisfaction of fulfilling a basic requirement. There has to be a predisposal—for example, thirsting for a lemonade on a hot summer day.

However, the 'predisposal' concerns other elements as well. It is not as simple as a 'need' which requires to be satisfied. Great messaging tiptoes into the subconscious and makes one favourably consider a product, service or offering. It plants a seed that sprouts and cracks open the ground of 'want'. Acting upon the latent desire or want, may require a nudge. And what I seek to emphasize is that the reams of data and analysis available will be more effective if they understand not just the behaviour, but also the backdrop, and use it in a more intricate and nuanced manner. The 'nudge' can be done effectively, through precise targeting and data, but the planting of the seed of new thought is not as straightforward and apparent as the available data makes it appear to be.

It is important to understand that when we stumble upon new ideas, thoughts and images, it does not happen in a state of preparedness. Often, it happens when one is not particularly looking for a new product and just browsing through life, and something unexpectedly catches the attention. This is well summarized by the Urdu word 'dafatan', which means 'all of a sudden'. This is how a new idea, product or concept tiptoes into the subconscious in a unique fashion; it is almost unachievable through calibrated means. Serendipity cannot be manipulated, only understood. It has the X factor, but even if one wants to understand it somewhat logically, it is not difficult. After all, one is more likely to get drawn in, if the defences are down. This is where the emotional connect of a brand subliminally comes into play.

> *Tiptoe messaging will plant the seed in the subconscious and one will create the rest themselves.*

By no means am I disregarding the precision possibilities of today's data-driven world, but it has to work in tandem with the 'tiptoe' messaging. Target messaging will garner attention and spur action when one is in a state of readiness. Tiptoe messaging will plant the seed in the subconscious and one will create the rest themselves. It is so powerful that it gives birth to everything around it—one will create the reason and the occasion themselves. The beautiful dress seen whilst window shopping, or fleetingly in an unrelated product's ad, could make one organize a grand celebration of a loved one's birthday, in order to have a reason for the purchase.

Hypertargeting—the narrow, focused and data-driven campaigns—is attractive to many a client. Given the steep sales targets, it's natural to try and seek prospects with the highest propensity to buy, but there is also a disadvantage in patterns. The assumption that the prospect's needs and aspirations are a given—that if every weekend, for two months, a certain brand of cereal is consumed, it will be so the next week too—leaves limited space for impulse and spontaneity. Sometimes, broadening the base is important. Keeping alive brand buzz—amongst priority and larger audience segments—creates saliency, which has significant long-term benefits.

This is not a case for mass media or casting the net wider, but of underlining that advertising is a science *and* an art. The science part involves data, and the 'tiptoe' part is the art. Be it storytelling, narrative idea, lighting, music or font—all that is consumed in a sensorial manner, is also part of subliminal consumption.

Brand and consumer-connect are shifting goalposts. Let's not miss the wood for the trees.

28

Good Begets Good:
Consumption with Compassion

A short while ago, the mundane need to buy a pair of shoes made me think of Blake Mycoskie's TOMS shoes. Business lore has it that about a decade ago, Mycoskie, on a visit to Argentina, was so affected by the plight of barefooted children that he went on to create a company that would match every pair of shoes bought with a new pair for a child in need.

This idea went on to evolve into a powerful business model, translating into a $300-million company, half of which Mycoskie sold in 2014. Last heard, this 'One for One' model—or, as I prefer to think of it, 'Consumption with Compassion' model—has been employed in companies selling other products such as spectacles.

That day, my train of thought was interrupted by a text message congratulating our company's performance at the Cannes Lions festival. 'Immunity Charm', an initiative created for the Afghan health ministry to tackle high infant mortality, had won a Grand Prix and several other awards. State Street Global Advisors's endeavour to have more women in boardrooms—the 'Fearless Girl', a bronze statue sculpted by Kristen Visbal, of a young girl boldly facing the charging bull at Wall Street—was also a winner. Both campaigns were from the stables of McCann Worldgroup's India and New York offices, respectively. Among other medal winners were: Channel 4's 'We're the Superhumans' campaign, aiming to change people's attitudes towards disabilities through the Paralympic Games; and Whirlpool's 'Care Counts', which underscored the direct correlation between a student's access to clean clothes and high school attendance. So, is 'being good' now a trend? Haven't mainstream brands been doing socially responsible work for years and showcasing them too? What is different now?

Till recently, social initiatives were considered part of the magnanimity of the company—its corporate social responsibility. Now, they are increasingly being considered essential, as they affect the core of the brand and are reflected in sales figures. The 'Inform-Entertain-Involve' model now has intrinsic value to contend with.

PASSION AND PURPOSE

From advertising being a one-way street where only brands reached out, today it's a consumer highway where brands are discussed in absentia. Consumer-to-consumer (C2C) discussions on how they choose products and brands in their social and political landscapes make it imperative for a brand to let grow ideas and germs of value. Moreover, in the product-marketer-brand and C2C communication algorithm, there is a newer voice gaining traction—that of the informed consumer. The mindset of the millennial is shaped uniquely. They are making and giving away money faster than any previous generation.

> *An additional price for ethical products is not hard to sell in this era.*

Millennials don't work just for a pay cheque but for a purpose. For them, the goal is not development of just the self but of their milieu, with 'work' and 'life' not compartmentalized but welded into one continuous existence. Businesses, for them, should respond to big issues like gender parity, child rights, environmental protection, etc. And many of them are willing to pay for the principle.

One of Nielsen's analyses shows increased sales for brands with sustainability claims on packaging. An additional price for ethical products is not hard to sell in this era. Sure, this is truer for the top rung of educated consumers, but it would be myopic to think that this trend would only trickle down gradually. In this age of social media, it could well be a torrent.

Add to this the fractured media landscape, which is being redefined as we speak. This hyper-connected world—where senses clash and converge—engages and embroils consumers in a mixed reality. There is also a trust deficit at play in the consumers' minds. The fluidity with which companies appear and disappear, be it e-commerce or mobile hardware, has the consumer looking for a modicum of certainty. And that assurance can come from a specific value system that is becoming essential for a brand to embody and exude.

In many cases, a certain tokenism has crept in: A pilot project without any intention of scaling it up; a limited-edition product; or a clever brand campaign. However, people can see through gimmicks, and these days, they can identify what is fake and exploitative, sooner.

It may also not be enough to think that 'doing good' in parts will instantly win over customers. If a brand's well-intended but shallow efforts are not in tune with the core values, a discordant note will soon become apparent.

The discerning will identify how the brand *is*, in terms of its products, services and marketing, and what it *portrays* through socially well-meaning initiatives. And if these are not in sync, the brand's equity will be diluted.

CLEAN CORPORATES

Brands are starting to incorporate integrity, transparency and sustainability into their overall approach. This is apparent in international food companies which talk of food with integrity and a mission to reduce waste stream to landfills by 50 per cent. Examples closer home are campaigns like a leading hygiene brand's 'Swachh Banega India' (let's make India clean) drive, which tackles a burning societal issue and entails investing and building cleanliness habits by partnering with the government; a food and drink brand that champions the cause of health by rooting out malnutrition in children; and a company that commits itself to environment-friendly production processes. These are easier said than done because they require not just symbolic gestures or one-off campaigns but changing the thought processes and systems of the company at the core. As the realization sets in, that today's consumer,

> *Investing in the 'good' for the long term allows a company to go beyond profits and shape a legacy.*

especially the millennials, are increasingly conscious of a product's impact on the society and environment, more and more companies are changing track to be in sync.

Investing in the 'good' for the long term, builds a relevant connect between the brand and its consumers in a larger social context. It allows a company to go beyond profits and shape a legacy that they want to leave behind.

Acknowledgements

Many of the essays that appear in this volume are versions of pieces that appeared in *The Economics Times, The Indian Express, Hindustan Times, Business World, India Today* and *Outlook*, to name a few of the publications that Prasoon Joshi contributes to. Every effort has been made to trace copyright holders and obtain permission to reproduce copyright material included in the book. In the event of any inadvertent omission, the publisher should be informed and formal acknowledgement will be included in all future editions of this book.